Brad Hunter is the national crime columnist for the *Toronto Sun*, prior to which he worked for the *New York Post*. Over a thirty-year career, his work has been published in newspapers and magazines all over the world. He has covered mafia hits, domestic murders and murderers who 'kill for kicks'. He has come face to face with killers such as mafia assassin Sammy 'The Bull' Gravano and Christa Pike, a teenager who tortured and murdered a love rival. He lives in Hamilton, Ontario, Canada and likes pubs, hockey, baseball and spending time with his family.

Also by Brad Hunter

Cold Blooded Murder

INSIDE THE MIND OF
JOHN WAYNE GACY

BRAD HUNTER

First published in 2022 by Ad Lib Publishers Ltd
15 Church Road
London SW13 9HE
www.adlibpublishers.com

Text © 2022 Brad Hunter

Paperback ISBN 978-1-802470-76-5
eBook ISBN 978-1-802470-88-8

Printed in the UK
10 9 8 7 6 5 4 3 2 1

Contents

CONTENTS

Prelude

'There are more victims,' Killer Clown detective says
By BRAD HUNTER,
NATIONAL CRIME COLUMNIST

TORONTO SUN, 29 March 2021

Rafael Tovar had developed a relationship with the corpulent killer sitting in the car with him.

The serial killer knew he couldn't lie to the veteran detective and with scores of bodies found in his suburban Chicago home, there wasn't much left to say.

But killer clown John Wayne Gacy couldn't help himself.

Tovar was one of the detectives who sent Gacy to death row after he was convicted of murdering thirty-three men and boys and burying their bodies in the basement crawl space of his home.

Gacy was iced via a needle in 1994.

Tovar told his tale to the *Toronto Sun* in the lead-up to a new four-part docuseries on the infamous killer.

'I honestly believe that he was honest with me. He was convinced that if you knew the answer or could find out, he'd tell you the truth,' Tovar said from his Chicago home.

'But he also liked to play mind games. So we're in the car and I ask him: "John, how many bodies are there?"' Tovar said, his Texas drawl still present after more than fifty years in Chicago.

Gacy paused.

'Then he replies, "I've told my lawyer and I've told you guys that there's thirty-three, but really, forty-five sounds like a good number,"' the retired detective recalled.

The detective – who logged more than thirty-nine years as a cop with the suburban Des Plaines, Ill., police department – believes Gacy and is certain there are more victims.

'I honestly believe there are more victims ... but the others might be outside Chicago. There's gaps in his killing when he was travelling,' Tovar said, adding, 'that doesn't mean he stops killing.'

Gacy was a contractor with ties to the Chicago Democratic Party machine and whose sinister alter egos were the clowns Pogo and Patches.

Beneath the veneer of respectability, he was a monster. He would pick up male hustlers and runaways and take them to his house before torturing, raping and murdering his victims.

Gacy would dispose of bodies in the unfinished basement of his home.

Tovar had worked narcotics before moving to homicide and recalled that the Gacy case came together quickly.

The beginning of the end started on the afternoon of 11 December 1978, when Gacy was discussing a contracting job with the owner of Nisson Pharmacy.

Part-time clerk Robert Piest, fifteen, overheard Gacy mention that he often hired teenage boys to work on his crews at $5 an hour. Piest wanted to talk to Gacy about a job.

At the maniac's home, Piest was tricked into wearing handcuffs.

As the boy began sobbing, Gacy told him: 'I'm going to rape you and you can't do anything about it.'

His terrified family told cops that he was last at Gacy's house. The Killer Clown's lies began unravelling.

As detectives scrambled to get a search warrant, Tovar spent time with Gacy at the cop shop.

'I had to entertain him while they got a search warrant, which wasn't going to be that hard,' Tovar said.

'You know, he spent the time bragging about himself, who he knew, just B.S.-ing. He was a loudmouth braggart and thought he was a big man in Cook County.'

He was, in the detective's words, a 'motormouth'. Gacy wouldn't shut up.

But when the search warrant finally came in, the Democratic machine man didn't want cops to mess up his house, so he told Tovar: 'Here's where the bodies are.'

'He told me, "I'm going to draw you guys a map of where all the bodies are buried," and that's what he did.'

Tovar said that he was 'stunned' at how casual the killer sitting across from him was. A chilling banality.

And that was it. Gacy told the detectives everything.

He was charged with thirty-three murders and went on trial on 6 February 1980. His defence team argued that the rotund monster was insane.

Five weeks later, he was convicted and it took the jury just two hours to sentence Gacy to die by lethal injection.

For his final meal, the former clown ordered a bucket of KFC, a dozen fried shrimp, french fries, fresh strawberries and a Diet Coke.

On 10 May 1994, Gacy was given the big adios.

Tovar called the serial killer the 'poster child for the death penalty'.

'John Gacy wasn't crazy. Even after he was executed, doctors studied his brain. There was nothing wrong with it,' Tovar said.

'He was just an evil bastard who enjoyed playing God. Gacy was the very personification of evil.'

1

Nameless but to God

On 6 August 1976, the light drizzle soaking Chicago was a welcome break from the temperatures that can make the Windy City a steam bath in the summertime. The thermometer sat at a comfortable seventy-two degrees.

America was on the move that bicentennial summer. The dual nightmares of Richard Nixon and the Vietnam War were in the past, and the energy crisis was also firmly in the rearview mirror. Young Americans were ready again to hit the road and see their country. They took trains, planes, buses, cars or used their thumbs to hitch-hike.

In those days, only a few academics and cutting-edge cops were using the chilling words 'serial killer'. Those sorts of lurid scare stories were reserved for the gaudy tabloids that lined the checkouts at supermarkets, newsstands and corner stores.

Particularly for young men, the nation's highways and byways offered a fun, no-risk adventure and an opportunity to discover the essence of a mythic America. One soldier in this army of the young was sixteen-year-old Jimmie Haakenson. Jimmie had been born in Chicago before his family moved to quieter St Paul, Minnesota when he was young. Jimmie, his family said, was a normal teenager who had a happy, settled childhood after his mother ditched his alcoholic father. He grew up in St Paul's Payne-Phalen neighbourhood on York Avenue. Everybody knew the kid. To put food on the table, his mother worked at a factory during the day, a sandwich shop at night and cleaned hotel rooms on the weekend for extra cash.

Yet Jimmie had a yearning for something different and unbeknownst to his family, he was planning on ditching St Paul. The smiling redhead wanted to explore the big city on his own. Chicago was 400 miles to the south-east and a world away. St Paul was staid, quiet, white and with none of the dangers and temptations of America's third largest city. On an August day in 1976, Jimmie suddenly announced to his sister: 'I'm going to Chicago.'

'Maybe he wanted to go back where he was born or something,' his sister Lorie said years later. 'Maybe he thought he'd see his dad.' How Jimmie got to Chicago, no one was quite sure. He may have taken a bus or, more likely, hitch-hiked. On 5 August 1976, Jimmie called his mother to let her know he had arrived safely in Chicago. He told her: 'I'm safe. I'm here, Mom. Don't worry.' His mother should have worried. The family never heard from him again. Detectives later suspected that, probably within hours of that fateful phone call, Jimmie was dead.

When his family didn't hear from him again, there was worry, sure. Maybe something terrible had happened to the boy with the mischievous smile. Or maybe the adventurous teenager was looking to start afresh somewhere else in his desire to leave his old life in Minnesota behind. There were a thousand possibilities, none of them were very palatable to his heartbroken family who subsequently spent decades looking for the answers that kept eluding them.

One terrifying possibility the family looked at, just three years after Jimmie vanished, was that he had fallen prey to notorious serial killer John Wayne Gacy. In fact, in 1979, his mother made the long trip to Chicago after the chubby contractor was arrested and accused of being America's worst serial killer. She was sick with worry that her boy was one of the bodies discovered in the makeshift crypt beneath Gacy's modest suburban home in Des Plaines outside Chicago.

The problem for the Haakenson family was that they did not have Jimmie's dental records. In those sunset years of the 1970s, dental records were one of the main tools in putting names to unidentified bodies so without them, identifying a decayed corpse could be almost impossible. The game-changing technology of DNA was at least a decade or more away.

'They definitely were a very concerned family,' Cook County Sheriff Tom Dart said. 'This was beyond horrific and they were very engaged, but at that point in time ... there wasn't even a notion that DNA was on the horizon. It was just, "If you don't have dental records, there's nothing we can do."'

Answers would never come for Jimmie's devastated mother, who died in 2008 without ever knowing what happened to her missing son.

Like Jimmie Haakenson, Francis Wayne Alexander was also missing for a long, long time – since some time between early 1976 and early 1977. The North Carolina man was about twenty-one years old at the time he disappeared. His mother, two half-sisters and two half-brothers always wondered what happened to the young man.

Alexander's family knew he had moved to the North Side of Chicago in 1975 and had been living there for about a year. He had been married in New York City and made his money working in bars and nightclubs. His half-sister, Carolyn Sanders – who described her brother as a 'jokester' who also had a sensitive side – later said she received a Christmas card from Alexander not long before he disappeared. 'Hey baby, I'll

13

see you soon cuz I love you. – Wayne,' it read. There was no return address. Sanders said she believed in her heart that her brother would keep his promise and visit – he always had. But the family never saw or heard from him again.

'Obviously we always held out hope that he would call or show up at our front doorstep,' his brother Clyde said in 2021. 'During the holidays, he was talked about. "Wow, wouldn't it be great to see Wayne during this Christmas?" or "What if he came in?"' Those holiday gatherings, weddings, birthdays and anniversaries would go on, but there would be no Wayne.

After not hearing from their brother for some time, the family suspected he may have moved to California. An attempt to file a missing persons report in the Golden State slammed headlong into a bureaucratic brick wall. No report was ever filed back in the Windy City.

While his family called him Wayne, detectives back in Chicago during the dark days of December 1978 had another name for him: Victim No. 5. There were eight murder victims whose identities would elude police for decades.

In 2011, Cook County Sheriff Tom Dart decided the time was right to do something about the unidentified remains recovered from the crawl space at a home at 8213 West Summerdale Avenue in the suburb of Des Plaines. Their killer unfortunately had the wherewithal to use acid and lime to dissolve the bodies, making identification significantly harder in those pre-DNA days. But time and technology were catching up to the runaway mystery that had now vexed investigators for more than three decades. One month after Dart announced the renewed push to bring closure to families whose agony and heartache had dragged on first for months then decades, his detectives had some answers.

The first John Doe identified was William George Bundy, previously known as Victim No. 19.

The sad tale of Bundy is chillingly familiar. He had vanished four days after his nineteenth birthday. Born on 22 October 1957 in Chicago, he wasn't a hayseed or a rube just off the turnip truck. He was a child of the city and knew its ways and its wickedness. Bundy was a local boy, a star diver and gymnast and a popular student at Chicago's Senn High School. After dropping out of high school, he worked construction jobs to make ends meet.

He disappeared on 26 October 1976. That autumn night, Bundy planned to go to a party with pals. Oddly, he forgot his wallet at home. He would never be seen alive again. Thirty-five years later, his sister Laura O'Leary still remembered the night she said goodbye to her brother. 'I remember him leaving that one night, saying he was going to a party and that was the last time I saw him,' she said.

Two years after Bundy's mysterious disappearance, the news about the suburban serial killer had exploded onto the nation's front pages and the revelations hit particularly hard at Gacy Ground Zero: Chicago. His family long suspected that Bundy may have fallen into the clutches of John Wayne Gacy. But they really didn't know for sure, just like other families desperate for answers. 'He [Bundy] was learning to be an electrician and when that happened and I found out that Gacy was a contractor, I just … I just knew it,' O'Leary said. But, even as the horrors emerged, the Bundy family could never prove that Bill had been a victim of this nondescript businessman.

'Bill's mother had come forward, seeking assistance. However, Bill's dentist had retired and the family proceeded to try to find [him],' Tom Dart later said. 'Once they did, they found that the dentist had destroyed all his dental records.'

In a grave marked 'We Remembered', Bundy's unidentified body was buried in 1981, alongside the remains of Gacy's other unidentified victims, as part of a public memorial at a cemetery in Hillside. Identity: Unknown but to God. Local funeral homes had paid for caskets, burial and headstones for the unidentified victims. In 2011, Cook County Sheriff Tom Dart was now determined to change the narrative for the doomed and unknown boys and young men.

Bundy's remains were exhumed in 2011. It was Laura who put the wheels in motion in the fall of 2011, cops would later admit. She called detectives. She had information about her brother. And she would provide a DNA sample.

The specimen was sent to a lab at the University of North Texas where they hit pay dirt with a match between O'Leary and the remains formerly known as Victim No. 19. Cops theorised that Bundy went to work for John Wayne Gacy's construction firm and, at some point, the apex predator developed sinister designs on the popular young man and decided to make his move.

'All my girlfriends wanted to date him. They didn't ever come over for me, only for him,' Laura told reporters about her brother in 2011. 'Today's terribly sad, but it is also a day that provides closure. We have been waiting for a long time for closure ... I know that the sorrow will eventually go away and I'll have a place to visit him.'

DNA finally brought some sense of closure to the Haakenson family as well and the next victim to be identified was Jimmie. Genetic material submitted by the teen's brother and sister confirmed the boy was one of Gacy's victims. It was Jimmie's nephew who became his uncle's advocate – even though he never met him. Investigators connected the dots from DNA and the Minnesota teen's original missing person report to determine that the boy with the sunny disposition who had been missing for so many years was, in fact, Victim No. 24.

'My brother has been missing for so long, and it's so nice to know that we've found our brother now, even though it's not good,' Jimmie's sister, Lorie, told the *Chicago Tribune*.

Sheriff Tom Dart told reporters at the time that the positive identification was bittersweet. 'It's beyond heartbreaking when you're explaining to them that their worst possible horrors are actually, unfortunately, true,' the cop said.

How young Jimmie fell into the clutches of an alpha-predator like Gacy will likely never be known. Maybe it was a job offer. Perhaps they met at the bus or train station or other areas where young men might be found. Gacy was known to prowl the Greyhound bus terminal looking for boys and there was no shortage of young men around this area who were alone in a strange city. Alone and vulnerable.

Hovering in the back of the minds of Jimmie's family over all these years, was the nightmarish scenario that the boy had fallen into the clutches of a homicidal maniac like John Wayne Gacy. 'This man was a horrible monster, and my brother somehow ran into him,' his sister told the *Tribune*. 'Somehow, on the bus or on a street corner, just being in the wrong place at the wrong time.' Jimmie wasn't the only kid or young man who was at the wrong place at the wrong time. There would be at least thirty-three of them.

More than four decades after his disappearance, Wayne's family was still looking for him. Sanders, his sister, scoured Facebook on the off-chance her brother's profile would appear. It didn't. In June 2021, cops asked the family for a DNA sample and any other germane information they had about their missing brother. What cops didn't say was that they suspected Alexander was the victim of a homicidal maniac. They didn't need to. In their hearts, the family had long suspected the absolute worst-case scenario. Francis Wayne Alexander was finally identified as Victim No. 5.

'We're just relieved that he has been found, even though it was such a tragedy in the way he was found and killed,' Richard Clyde, Alexander's half-brother, told the *Chicago Sun-Times*. 'We're just trying to process it all. It's very difficult.'

Carolyn Sanders, his sister, was just fourteen when her big brother Wayne vanished and said the family believed 'something was preventing him from contacting [the family]'. 'My initial thought was Gacy, and with that going through your head of your sibling, it's excruciating,' she told the *Sun-Times*. 'I don't think any of us ever felt that he didn't want to talk to us … I know he's suffered, I'm sure, but he's not suffering any more. It's just a process I guess you have to deal with the best way a person possibly can.'

* * * *

Like the horrors of war, disaster and other monstrosities of the human experience, the nightmare that emerged in suburban Chicago on a December day in 1978 has seemed without end. Not just for the victims and their families but for cops, prosecutors and the world at large. The Gacy story is like a boot to the face and a nauseating jolt in the stomach at the bitter reality that there are demons among us whose cruelty is almost otherworldly.

Although the families of the victims and the survivors expressed gratitude and relief to finally know the fates of the young men who had gone unidentified for so long, in some ways, it was another triumph for John Wayne Gacy. Planted nearly three decades ago, his power to terrify has seemed eternal, outlasting his murder frenzy by decades.

Knowing the truth has brought little relief to the Alexander and Haakenson families. 'It is hard, even forty-five years later, to know the fate of our beloved Wayne. He was killed at the hands of a vile and evil man,' his sister said. 'Our hearts are heavy and our sympathies go out to the other victims' families. Our only comfort is knowing this killer no longer breathes the same air as we do. We can now lay to rest what happened and move forward by honouring Wayne.'

Lorie Sisterman echoes Sanders and is grateful her mother never knew Jimmie's true fate. 'I'm glad my mom is already gone, so that she didn't find out the awful things that happened to her son, but then she went to her grave not knowing where her son was,' Sisterman said in 2017. Perhaps believing he had simply left and begun a new life was easier.

Now, there are five John Does still left to identify. Their bodies had been crudely stashed in the crawl space under the suburban ranch home after dying in the most horrific manner imaginable.

John Wayne Gacy departed this world for a one-way ticket to hell on 10 May 1994, courtesy of a blast of a lethal cocktail at the hands of the State of Illinois. But, instead of easing into well-deserved obscurity, Gacy and his chilling ethos remains like the stench of living next to a dump. On a yearly basis new sordid details and breakthroughs emerge in a case that was essentially closed when the Killer Clown was executed.

Detectives who worked the Gacy investigation and, indeed, many criminologists are convinced that the serial killer's death tally exceeded the thirty-three victims he copped to torturing, raping and killing. Did he kill before 1972 when, aged thirty, he claimed to have murdered his first known victim? And what about his many moves over the years? In his home office, John Wayne Gacy had a map of the United States. It was filled with pins representing the places he had lived or visited. 'There were pins all over the place,' retired FBI profiler Robert Ressler later said. 'I think Gacy's good for more than thirty-three.'

Cops in scores of jurisdictions around the Midwest and the rest of America have victims – often unidentified – who might fit Gacy's modus operandi: young, male, alone and vulnerable. During Gacy's homicidal apex, young men weren't even aware that people like John Wayne Gacy existed. Even movies and television had not caught on to the emerging phenomenon of the serial killer.

As Cook County Sheriff's detectives struggled to identify the unidentified victims in 2011, they discovered, buried in the depths of their evidence room, two vials of John Wayne Gacy's blood. These have been entered into the national DNA data bank. One day they may tie the killer to other cold-case homicides which detectives suspect, in their guts, he may be responsible for.

There were twenty-nine bodies in the crawl space and on his property. Four more would be dumped into the Des Plaines River after he ran out of space in the DIY crypt he had created beneath his home. But Gacy claimed he dumped *five* bodies into the river. When Gacy claimed forty-five kills, retired detective Rafael Tovar believed him. It was just the sort of person Gacy was.

By his own twisted nature, Gacy has ensured that his dark countenance will endure not just in books, podcasts, movies and in TV documentaries, but as a real life bogeyman, who remains an enigma. While Gacy got the needle to oblivion in 1994, he put the pieces in place that ensured his twisted chess game with detectives and grieving families would roll on well after he was seated with a one-way ticket on an express train to hell.

2

This Boy's Life

The boozing started early on 17 March 1942 among denizens of Chicago who traced their heritage to Ireland. A lot of others, who wished they were Irish, were also ready to join in the alcohol-fuelled fun. It was fifty-five degrees with a light rain that St Patrick's Day on the cusp of spring.

There were a lot of reasons for Americans to be drinking that day. While the Great Depression that had ravaged America's industrial heartland was in the past and the factories were booming, a new existential crisis had shaken the nation to its core. On 7 December 1941, Japanese planes obliterated the U. S. Pacific Fleet at Pearl Harbor and suddenly the nation was at war. Four months into the fighting and the situation was dire for America and her allies. Great Britain and her dominions of Canada and Australia had their backs against the wall in Europe, Africa and now, Asia.

America – a country that worships winners – was watching its forces being obliterated across the Pacific in places most of their countrymen had never heard of. Wake Island, Guam, Hong Kong and all points in between were falling to the relentless Japanese juggernaut. Worse, U. S. and Filipino forces were now trapped on the Bataan Peninsula in the Philippines without supplies, food or ammunition, and simply waiting for the inevitable collapse that would come. This would come on 19 April 1942 with the capture of 76,000 American and Filipino prisoners.

On that St Paddy's Day a world away, General Douglas MacArthur took a patrol torpedo boat for Australia with his family and abandoned his men fighting for their lives on Bataan.

But for the family who lived at 4505 North Marmora Avenue in Chicago, the woes of the world were the least of their concerns that day. A couple was about to add a new child to a suddenly very dangerous and uncertain world.

At the time, the Jefferson Park neighbourhood on the Northwest Side was the redoubt of Eastern European families, particularly Polish and Ukrainians. The area was annexed by the city in 1889 and was initially settled by German immigrants. So far on the edge of the growing and bustling metropolis was this neighbourhood, that a sign was erected signalling that visitors were at the 'Gateway to Chicago'. The neighbourhood's showpiece and namesake is, in fact, Jefferson Park, which is now listed on the National Register of Historic Places.

Notoriously taciturn U. S. Vice-President Dick Cheney visited the neighbourhood during the 2000 presidential election and attended the annual Polonia Festival, where he danced the polka and served party-goers with kielbasa, stuffed cabbage and beer. And as the crowd cheered, Cheney shouted in Polish, '*Sto lat*'(May you live to see a hundred years) to loud cheers. Even today, visitors could be forgiven if they thought they were in Warsaw. But Cheney's visit aside, the area has long been a Democratic Party stronghold with wide support from city and Cook County workers, cops, firefighters and others who have lived in the area for decades. And, in spite of the violent crime wave throttling Chicago, Jefferson Park was a safe neighbourhood in 1942 and remains so today.

That St Paddy's Day in Chicago in 1942, America was in a war it was clearly losing. But in the numerous movie theatres that then dotted the landscape there was hope in the preservation of American values. Across the silver screen, John Wayne strode like a colossus. Whipping the Indians. Whipping the Japanese. Now John Wayne ... there was a man. As John Stanley Gacy saw it, Wayne was the epitome of what it meant to be an American male.

John Stanley Gacy's first and only son was about to be born that day, and he thought the name John Wayne Gacy had a nice, masculine ring to it. John Stanley was born in Chicago on 20 June 1900 as the terrible new century was still in embryonic form. His parents were Nicholas Gacy and Veronika Jablonski, whose heritage was Danish and Polish – a fitting mix for Jefferson Park.

For John Stanley Gacy, the seminal moments of his life that would lay the foundations of horror to come many, many decades later happened across the Atlantic Ocean in France. On 6 April 1917, the United States officially entered the First World War and John Stanley Gacy felt obliged to do his duty, so enlisted in the U. S. Army. Something must have happened on the killing fields of Europe as it did for millions of other men in the 'war to end all wars' because Gacy returned home to Chicago in 1919 a very changed man.

Suddenly, booze became a problem for a man who, by the standards of the time, became quite successful as a mechanical engineer at an automobile assembly plant. Other accounts have described him as a mechanic. Despite his issues with alcohol, he was successful and prosperous even as the Great Depression saw millions of jobs disappear, throwing 25% of the U. S. workforce onto welfare rolls.

Little else is known about John Stanley Gacy during those hardscrabble years. What *is* known is that on 7 January 1939, the long-time bachelor married pharmacist Marion Elaine Robinson. She was born on 4 May 1908 in Racine, Wisconsin, about ninety minutes north of Chicago. In November of that year, the couple gave birth to a daughter they named Joanne Ruth. And on 17 March 1942, the Gacys welcomed their second child and only son, John Wayne Gacy, at Edgewater Hospital, where future first lady Hilary Rodham Clinton would be born five years later. Various reports say the baby boy was born with a congenital heart defect later diagnosed as an enlarged heart. Another sister, Karen, would follow making a family of five.

Yet the joy a new baby boy brought didn't seem to soothe the emotional chaos roiling inside deeply troubled John Stanley Gacy. His boozing became steadily worse. Now forty-two years old, on a nightly basis he would retreat to the basement of the neat brick, three-bedroom bungalow on North Marmora. And he would then proceed to stupify himself with booze while having imaginary conversations with long-gone army buddies who perished in France. No one in his family ever knew what state John Stanley Gacy would be in, but when he went to the basement, the family knew what was coming next. Behind the prosperity and fine, neat home there was turmoil in the Gacy household causing the family to walk on a knife-edge at all times. Early on, as a toddler, John Wayne Gacy would watch as his father battered his mom, once even seeing John Stanley knocking out his wife's dental crowns. What he could not have known was that his turn was coming.

In 1992, John Wayne Gacy himself was more philosophical about his long-dead father rather than being bitter or angry about the lousy hand he had been dealt in the parenting department.

'My dad was domineering,' Gacy told CBS Chicago. 'He had a different set of values, but he was also a very stern individual. My dad drank a lot, and when he drank a lot, he was abusive to my mother and to me. But I never swung at my dad, because I loved him for what he stood for.'

The young Gacy was turning out to be a major disappointment to his father. While his namesake was wiping the floor with Nazis and the Japanese in blockbusters like *Flying Tigers*, *Back to Bataan* and *The Fighting Seabees*, John was overweight and unathletic. Making matters worse, as John Stanley saw things in his domestic kingdom, because of the heart condition his son had had since birth, he was to avoid all sports at school. The boy was of no use when it came to the myriad home-improvement projects his father was always working on. In John Stanley Gacy's eyes, his son was a 'sissy' and, even worse, the boy was 'dumb and stupid'. Worse, he'd dress in his mother's underwear. Adding insult, John Stanley slammed his son as a 'mama's boy' who would more than likely 'grow up queer'.

So John soon became the target of his father's violence. And it was in the basement – where his father kept his workshop – that the child was verbally humiliated and emotionally tortured. Gacy himself recalled his father beating him with a leather belt after he accidentally disarranged the components of a car engine his father was working on. When he was in Grade 4, John Wayne began to experience blackouts. While there may have been a medical component to these spells, the torment he endured at the hands of his father no doubt accentuated them. When his mother tried to intervene to protect young John Wayne, she would feel the fury of her husband's fist.

Many boys – particularly of Gacy's generation – suffered beatings and verbal and emotional abuse. The vast majority would go on to lead productive, normal lives with a steely determination to be better parents than the men who had crushed their young souls. Criminologist Christopher Berry-Dee, who wrote a book on the childhoods of serial killers, said that Gacy's abusive background will still never explain what would come decades later. '[Millions of kids get beaten] but that doesn't make them serial killers,' Berry-Dee told A&E True Crime. 'You have three children who suffered the same abuse, but only one turned out to be the rotten apple.'

Marion Gacy on the other hand, loved the boy, as did his sisters. His mother called him 'Johnny' until the day he died. Her boy was smart, did well in school and was charming. Her husband saw none of it. Her love 'was his only nurturing'.

Dr. Richard Rappaport, who served as the chief psychiatrist for John Wayne Gacy's defence, spent sixty-five hours interviewing Gacy to try to save his life. In Rappaport's eyes, the traumatic experiences the young Gacy suffered at the hands of his father were something that no child should endure. It was, Rappaport opined, the central instrument in the future killer's 'mental and emotional dysfunction'.

'The relationship that went on between the two of them [Gacy and his father] was the forerunner for the relationship he had to his victims,' Rappaport said, years later. The crawl space under Gacy's home, that became his personal chamber of horrors, harked to those dark days as a child in his father's basement: a place of fear, foreboding and soul-crushing humiliation. Even his methodology echoed back to his dark childhood, Rappaport said. There were the handcuffs rendering the victims helpless. And, like a comic-book super-villain, Gacy would tell them exactly how he was going to torture and ultimately, kill them. Then he would force them to beg for their lives.

'He was putting on a scenario that re-enacted the way he felt as a child,' Rappaport said. 'He was essentially getting them to play his role, of being helpless … while he played the role of the father. And he'd punish them for begging, and for looking like cowards – whatever he felt about his own inadequacies, he put on them.'

During his last years, while on death row, Gacy began writing something of a manuscript that would cover every year of his life. According to a 1994 *New Yorker* article, some of the entries are brief, others extensive. He wrote about one of the seminal events in his life which occurred when he was five years old. It is entitled: 'Background incident, age five, John W. Gacy, sexual bewilderment, 1947'.

These are the killer's own words.

Back then, in the summer, after Dad was off to work, and mother had things in order at the house she would visit some of the neighbourhood woman friends with children. Anyway, this particular time we had all went down to another family's house which was in the next block south on Opal. We would usually stay for lunch, and get back home by three p.m.

The family's kids were all older than the three of us, except for two which were our age. From what I could remember, several of their children were slow learners, and one was mentally retarded, so she stayed close to home. While the rest of the kids were either playing or taking a nap after lunch, this older girl said that she would watch over me and we went upstairs. She was mentally retarded, and fifteen at the time. While playing house in one of the bedrooms she took off all my clothes and was fondling me and tickling me, me being too young to know what was going on. Downstairs, both their mother and Mom thought that the kids were too quiet and went to investigate, and starting to account for them. When they came upstairs, walked into the room where we were, they saw her playing with my ding-a-ling. And their mother while yelling came in and grabbed the girl, and hit her several times, while yelling about what she was up to. My mother came over to me, asked me what I was doing with my clothes off or something to that nature, and got me dressed and took me downstairs. I was scared, as I thought that I would get hit too. I was told not to be taking my clothes off with girls and to sit down there by them until they left. I had told them that the girl said it was all right for her to take my clothes off.

He observed: 'While I never did understand what we were doing that was so wrong at the time, it left a profound feeling on me in my thinking about taking off clothes in front of others, even my sisters, thinking that I was going to get hit for doing it. As at the time I was told that what we were doing was dirty and wrong. I think now all it was curiosity, me not knowing, and her for her age, even being retarded.' The shocked Gacy family severed their relationship with the family.

The year 1950, was another watershed in the turbulent life of the chubby, unpopular boy. It's during this year that he recalls being abused once more, this time by a much older man who had befriended his father. He recounts this incident in the manuscript too. This entry is entitled: '1950, age eight, Sexual incident with contractor'.

In the late spring of 1950, we lived at 3536 North Opal, in Chicago, Ill., at that time there was an empty lot next door on the right. And word was that a new house was to be built. After the foundation was poured, a contractor came around and was looking at the lot. Since it was a Saturday, my dad was in the yard trimming hedges. The contractor spoke with my dad and one thing led to another and dad offered him a beer, and they sat in our yard and talked. Mother came out, so he met her too. I was playing in the yard, and was interested in the conversation about building. Several weeks passed, and the contractor was back to see how progress was going on his building (weekday). He seen me in the yard as we kids were home for spring vacation. He asked me if I would like to go and see some other building sites, and have some ice cream. I asked mom and she said it was all right. (I must add at the first visit with my parents, they talked about wrestling on TV.) I went with the man in his car and after the second stop, he asked me if I had seen last week's wrestling show, I said yes, and then he said that he wanted to show me a new hold in the car. He moved out from behind the steering wheel, closer to me, and told me to bend down and put my head under his leg, which I did, he held me between his legs for several minutes, tightly so that I could not move, and in fact I had tears in my eyes. When he seen that, he let me go, and said let's go get that ice cream I told you about. After that I returned home, never mentioning anything about it. Couple weeks went by, he came back, seen me and asked if I would like to go again with him to get ice cream, again went. After several stops he was talking about wrestling, and again he wants to show me a new hold, so we did it again in the car, only it was the same hold, with a little more grabbing of me between the legs. Ice cream again and I was dropped off at the house. After a fourth time of the same thing each time when I seen him coming down the street, I ran and hid from him. Later, my mother is in the yard and told me that the contractor was looking for me. I told her I didn't like that man, and didn't want to go with him. She said he wanted to take me for ice cream for watching over his building. I told her I didn't care. When my dad came home that night, mom told him what happened, and dad came to me and asked me about it. I told him what was happening each time, and he told me that he didn't want me going with him no more. The next time he came around on a Saturday, my dad was home, I stayed in the house. Dad went over and talked with him, and from what I can understand from hearsay, Dad told this man to stay away from me or he would call the police. With that he was around a few more times to see his building finished, but never came near our house again. That's all that happened, but I have never forgotten it from the age of eight and a half. I still remember the man wasn't too tall, middle-aged, semi-bald, dark heavy glasses, with a moustache, a little overweight, two-door car, light blue, I think it was a new Chevy, it was newer than my dad's, as in 1950 he had a 46 Chevrolet four-door.

In 1950, John Stanley Gacy had discovered that his son and another boy had been caught sexually fondling a young girl. The result for John Wayne was a severe whipping with a razor strop at the hands of his raging father.

Years later, Gacy's younger sister Karen, told Oprah Winfrey in an interview, that the future killer and his sisters learned to 'toughen up against the beatings' and that 'John wouldn't cry while he was being beaten.' Still, Rappaport said that while Gacy was emotionally and physically abused by his father, he exhibited none of the signs that have come to be known as markers for serial killers. There was no bed-wetting, fire-setting and he did not torture small animals. These three characteristics are called the Macdonald Triad after a 1963 study by psychiatrist Dr. J. M. Macdonald.

'I spent a full year [before evaluating him] studying the literature, trying to understand how a guy who seemed so normal could be so abnormal in this one respect,' Rappaport said.

But one other incident may have played a role in Gacy's development and his ultimately murderous nature. When he was eleven years old, in 1953, he was hit in the head by a metal swing in a local playground. The injury caused the boy to suffer a blood clot in the brain that was not diagnosed until he was sixteen years old. In the interim, he began suffering from the fainting spells and blackouts that his father believed were a ruse, a bid for sympathy or simply part of his suspected effeminate nature. His mother, sisters and friends knew that John Wayne was not faking. That did not matter a whit to his father who continued to show nothing but contempt for the boy. Even as the young boy lay sick in a hospital bed – where he spent most of a year – John Stanley Gacy ranted and raved at his bedside.

Gacy would later estimate that between the time he was fourteen and eighteen years old he lost a year of his education, being treated for his enlarged heart, the fainting spells and a burst appendix.

Age did not seem to temper the always simmering rage of John Stanley Gacy. One of John Wayne Gacy's high-school friends recalled the numerous incidents when the old man would suddenly snap and then proceed to batter his only son without the slightest provocation. Once, in 1957, the friend watched as John Stanley exploded, drunk, from his basement lair to suddenly begin verbally laying into John Wayne, belittling and humiliating him, before beating his boy senseless for no apparent reason. His appalled mother Marion tried to intervene. John Wayne would just 'put up his hands to defend himself' but even as he got older and bigger, he never lashed out at his father during one of these heartbreakingly frequent incidents.

As he sat rotting on death row, and the inevitable crept closer, John Wayne Gacy remained steadfast in defending his cruel father. 'My dad has been butchered,' he told a writer for *The New Yorker*. 'The media made an image out of him like he was an alcoholic monster. Okay, my dad drank, and he was Jekyll and Hyde when he drank. If he came up from the basement and said the walls were pink, you said the walls were pink, but you learned to stay away from him and keep your mouth shut at the dinner table.'

Gacy then extolled the old man's values. 'This is my first pair of Levi's,' he said of his prison pants. 'When I grew up, my father always said that corduroys and khakis were the proper way for a man to dress. If you were wearing jeans, you were making sexual gestures. I went to school in flannel shirts and corduroy pants.

'But I never hated my father. He was a strong man. He married my mother when he was forty-one. We didn't get along. I thought I could never please him, but I still love him. If we went fishing, though, like we did for a week every summer, and I rocked the boat, or my line got tangled, or it happened to rain, Jesus, it was all my fault.'

When the writer suggested that Gacy's father was a coward and a bully, the doomed killer bristled.

'I learned values from my father,' Gacy said. Then he paused and recalled some flagstones he had used his bike to move were still in place at the original family home. And the tree he had planted as a boy? It still stood. Nothing his father had done remained.

'My way to remember my dad is not to be like him,' he said. 'That's my way of getting back at the son of a bitch.'

3

1978 – The River

Finding a floater in the Des Plaines River was not unusual. It was accidental drowning for some while others were driven to despair – left without options or hope – and took the plunge off one of the numerous bridges that span the waterway.

The river stretches about 133 miles from Racine County in southern Wisconsin through northern Illinois and into urban Cook County and suburban Chicago. Eventually, the Des Plaines meets the Kankakee River that then forms the Illinois River, which is a tributary of the Mississippi River.

On 30 June 1978, authorities found the body of a young man whose remains were caught near the Dresden Island Lock and Dam in the Illinois River. Cops suspected that the body had been thrown from a bridge on the busy I-55 highway that stretches from Chicago to Houston, Texas. The victim had no identification. The body in the river was naked with one identifying marker: an arm tattoo that read 'Tim Lee'. A similar young man had been known to frequent the gay bars on the city's North Side, but it would take almost six months to identify the body and, by then, detectives would be buried in corpses, the likes of which the world had never seen outside a war zone.

Earlier that month, twenty-year-old Timothy O'Rourke had left his Chicago apartment to get cigarettes and never returned. A missing persons report was filed with Chicago Police. Pals said O'Rourke was known to frequent gay bars in Bughouse Square. John Wayne Gacy was also known to prowl the seedy watering holes looking for action with young men. In fact, O'Rourke told his roommate that he had recently met a contractor on Chicago's Northwest Side who had offered him a job.

Grundy County authorities asked the Illinois Bureau of Criminal Identification to compare the fingerprints lifted off 'Tim Lee' with any they may have had on file for one Timothy Rourke.

In the course of making routine calls, a crime reporter for the *Chicago Sun-Times* told his detective contacts he had found O'Rourke's dad. The worried father told the reporter that his son was interested in karate. Martial arts legend Bruce Lee, star of *Enter the Dragon* and scores of other kung fu classics, was his favourite movie star. And the father later confirmed to detectives that his son had a tattoo that read 'Tim Lee'. Dental records and X-rays confirmed the cops' suspicions: the floater was Timothy O'Rourke.

After it emerged that O'Rourke was the victim, Chicago detective Jerry Lawrence received a phone call from the victim's roommate, transwoman Donita Ganzon. She recognised the description of the 'Tim Lee' tattoo. Donita also informed the detective that she knew that a contractor on the Northwest Side had offered O'Rourke a job just before his disappearance. The contractor's name was Gacy. But then Timothy had had some misgivings. He thought, Ganzon said, that maybe Gacy was giving him the runaround and leading him on. When Ganzon asked her roommate: 'Is this Gacy gay?', O'Rourke had just smiled at her.

The world had not yet heard of John Wayne Gacy. He was known to people in the neighbourhood where he lived and in local Democratic Party circles where he had become something of a player. To the world at large, he still remained a nobody. Within six months, that would change. Everyone would know the name John Wayne Gacy.

In 1978, the rotund contractor had a problem. He was running out of room in the crawl space underneath his house – 8213 West Summerdale Avenue in suburban Des Plaines – where he had been stashing the bodies of young men and boys like kindling. Gacy later told detectives he had considered storing the bodies of his brutalised victims in his attic, but then thought better of it, worrying that leakage might be a serious problem. Instead, he had decided to dump his recent victims into the Des Plaines River.

Frank Landingin, nineteen, was a troubled kid who had been in and out of tangles with the law. He was familiar with the seedier side of the street. He had last been seen by pals on 4 November 1978. Eight days later on 12 November 1978, he was discovered floating in the Des Plaines River.

The coroner quickly ascertained that Landingin hadn't drowned and there were all the telltale signs that he was a murder victim. The cause of death was determined to have been asphyxiation. Stuffed into his mouth were his own briefs. The medical examiner ruled that he had been strangled to death and had inhaled his own regurgitation as a result of the blockage. In addition, the autopsy revealed that the young man had eaten within ninety minutes of his demise. And Landingin had eaten very well indeed, the medical examiner opined. Bean sprouts indicated that the victim had probably had Chinese food for his final meal. Plus, he had recently had sexual relations as his seminal vesicles had been emptied.

Cops learned that on the night he disappeared, Landingin had been released from the Cook County Jail after making bond on a battery charge. The young Chicago man's criminal record wasn't pretty. He had been arrested several times for assault and auto theft. More recently, he had been accused of assaulting his girlfriend.

Detectives discovered that, after Landingin made bail, he met his father Francisco at a North Side watering hole. He told the old man, he was going to look for his girlfriend and try to apologise and make up for what he had done. The troubled young man was last seen walking west on Chicago's Foster Avenue around three a.m.

It was later revealed that Landingin was the thirteenth young man to choke to death on his own underwear in the Chicago area.

Not three weeks after the disappearance of Landingin, James Mazzara, twenty-one, enjoyed a Thanksgiving feast with his family. It would be the last hurrah of a heartbreakingly short life. Mazzara was a little guy, with brown hair. He had grown up in the Windy City suburb of Elmwood Park. At Thanksgiving dinner, he told his family that he was working in construction and doing fine.

Mazzara had been living with pals on Clark Street – the same street where the St Valentine's Day Massacre had occurred in 1929 – but when he arrived home one day in later November 1978, he discovered he had been evicted. The apartment was located about three blocks from the notorious red-light district of Bughouse Square. He was last seen walking in the direction of Bughouse Square, carrying a suitcase. After they reported James's disappearance, Mazzara's tight-knit family would later check out a rough-trade bar where he hung out.

Detectives asked the family if he had any nicknames. Yeah, sure, they said: 'Mo-Jo.' On his way to prison, John Wayne Gacy told investigators his penultimate victim was some kid named 'Something-Joe' from the Elmwood Park neighbourhood.

Mazzara's body was later pulled from the Des Plaines River, less than a mile from where the body of Timothy O'Rourke had been discovered. He had been strangled to death with a ligature.

There were now three boys that had been found in the river.

In 1978, Gacy had been getting away with murder for a long time. Why didn't anyone make the connection? Did the cops blow it? There were many reasons and geography and communication were among them.

Policing was less sophisticated and Los Angeles homicide detectives at the time were experiencing similar jurisdictional headaches during their hunt for killers like the Night Stalker, the Hillside Strangler and the Freeway Killer. The serial murders plaguing Los Angeles and southern California at the time were something detectives had never seen before.

'There is no question southern California was in a state of panic. We would always say, "Please, God, not another one,"' veteran homicide detective Bob Grogan told the author in 2021. 'Forty-four years later I still have dreams about the victims and I still want to say, "Don't open that door."'

At the time there was no DNA testing, there were no mobile phones, very few computers and the computers that the police did have were archaic. Most problematic was the lack of co-operation between the scores of law enforcement agencies that speckled the sunny landscape of the Golden State. Los Angeles spans nearly a hundred square miles, and it is not just the domain of the LAPD, but the L. A. County Sheriffs and numerous smaller police departments. At the time, the detectives didn't realise it, but they were revolutionising complex investigations. And egos did get in the way.

'A woman is grabbed off the street in Los Angeles, murdered elsewhere, then dumped in another jurisdiction. That can make things very complicated,' Grogan said.

In Chicago, Gacy would often pick up the boys near Bughouse Square then take them to his house of horrors in suburban Des Plaines, in a totally different jurisdiction. And many of the victims were runaways from the Chicago area, but others came from across the Midwest and points beyond.

Retired Des Plaines Police detective Michael Albrecht, who Gacy ended up taking a liking to, echoed the frustrations of his California counterparts. Time and technology were antagonists in the Gacy investigation. Albrecht got to know Gacy very well. He was part of a four-man team who were watching the killer around the clock as they closed in on him. Albrecht was there when Gacy confessed and when he drew the insidious diagram of where he had buried the bodies.

'At that time, Chicago's districts were somewhat independent of each other. Things were more local, and society wasn't as vocal as it is now. So, I mean, there could have been more done,' Albrecht told *Esquire* magazine in 2021. In addition, there was no central database or VICLAS (Violent Crime Linkage Analysis System) that could potentially link the crimes. It was all done on gut instinct.

'The problem was communication and that's something I worry about today. In the old days, we would meet our colleagues in other departments for a coffee in the morning or a beer in the evening,' retired detective Tom Lange said. 'You had a better read of what was going on when you met face to face rather than a stranger sending an email. Today, they're well-intentioned, but a different breed. We'd have to keep a roll of quarters and keep our eyes peeled for a phone booth.'

'Back in the seventies, you didn't have a computer system like now. I mean, where you could do a lot of research on things,' Albrecht told *Esquire*. 'And, unfortunately, now I'm not making excuses for anybody, but there were a lot of runaways at the time. Kids were constantly running away. And what happened a lot of times – there was either a fight with their parents; girlfriend, boyfriend problems – whatever it may be. And they'd run away, and the next day they'd be home. In fact, one of the results that came out of the Gacy case was that any juvenile that was reported missing had to be immediately entered into the criminal justice system.'

Still, Gacy was not a completely unknown commodity to law enforcement. There had been police reports over the years including two in 1978. In early January, a nineteen-year-old man had gone to the Cook County Sheriff's with a harrowing story. Just a little past midnight, he told officers, a man had pulled his car to the curb, blocking his path. The beefy man behind the wheel then pointed a handgun at the boy and said he was a cop. Then he handcuffed the kid before ordering him into the car. The man was John Wayne Gacy.

More horror would follow when they got to Gacy's modest suburban bungalow. There, he raped the teen and then stuck the weapon point-blank against the boy's face and began spinning the chamber of the .38-calibre handgun as if engaging his terrified victim in a game of Russian roulette. Gacy pulled the trigger numerous times before one of the blanks in the chamber went off. Gacy then choked the boy out and held his head underwater in a filthy bathtub. His victim kept losing consciousness. By then, the boy was in agonising pain and begging his tormentor to kill him, but his attacker wasn't quite through with the teen. The torture went on through the night. But, instead of killing the boy, in the morning, Gacy drove the unnamed victim to work.

When detectives came to question the well-known contractor, he told them that there was an explanation for the whole incident. The boy, Gacy explained, was a hustler and they'd made an agreement to have sadomasochistic sex. The teen was pissed off because the businessman wouldn't pay him. That's why he went to the cops. In the end, the assistant state's attorney decided Gacy would appear more believable in court than his teenaged victim and the charges were dropped.

But like many sexual predators, Gacy could not help himself and would not be deterred. Even a close call like the incident with the teenager failed to slow his pursuit of violent, non-consensual sex – and murder. In May of 1978, Gacy once more came close to the edge when a civil warrant was issued for him.

This time, a twenty-six-year-old man named Jeffrey Rignall claimed that the contractor offered him a ride to a bar. But once inside his Oldsmobile, Gacy quickly covered Rignall's face with a rag soaked in chloroform. Rignall passed out. Predictably, Gacy took him to the home where he was always most comfortable – his lair, his chamber of horrors, his crypt.

Rignall's arms and head were restrained in a pillory device attached to the ceiling. His feet were locked into another contraption. Gacy informed the terrified young man that he was in complete control. He, Gacy, would do whatever he wanted to Rignall. For hours, the serial killer unleashed a catalogue of depravity on Rignall. He tortured then raped Rignall using random items, including lit candles and whips. When he needed a break, he would again chloroform Rignall until he passed out. But again, for some reason, Gacy didn't kill him.

When the stunned victim woke up the next morning, he found himself at the base of a statue near where Gacy had picked him up. His pants were undone and his rectum was bleeding. Rignall's partner, Ron Wilder, said he was bleeding, sick and covered in rope burns. He also had chloroform burns all over his face. Rignall went to the police.

But the police didn't seem interested in taking Rignall's account seriously as they stood over his hospital bed. Retired Judge of the Circuit Court of Cook County William Kunkle called the tale 'vague' and he added that, since the victim didn't know where Gacy's house was, 'it was a very minimalist police report and nothing transpired.'

In the four-part documentary *John Wayne Gacy: The Devil in Disguise*, Wilder claimed the cops' indifference was down to the fact that Rignall was gay. 'The police assumed that Jeff's encounter with Gacy was a consensual arrangement,' he said in the 2021 documentary. 'They had no clue of how to treat a gay rape of any sort and did not even think that would be possible.'

But Rignall was not about to take the horrendous attack on him lying down. 'Jeff thought that man could kill somebody so he figured whatever he did to him, he was going to do it to other people,' Wilder said. 'That's why he wanted to catch him.'

Rignall remembered the black Oldsmobile, taking the Kennedy Expressway and he remembered some of the side streets. So, he and two friends, including Wilder, staked out the Cumberland exit of the Expressway. He didn't know his attacker's name or anything else about him but he did know the car and a rough idea of what the plate numbers on the Oldsmobile were. And he knew the home where he was held prisoner was near an airport because he kept hearing planes during his ordeal.

In April 1978, Rignall finally spotted the Oldsmobile and Gacy was arrested on 15 July 1978 and charged with battery against the man he had ravaged. But he was quickly released on a low bond. The charge would still be pending when Gacy was arrested in December 1978.

When Rignall and Wilder begged to have the charges bumped up, they were allegedly met with homophobic hyperbole from the state attorney. Gacy's connection, successful business, societal standing and popularity in the community gave him a shield that he used effectively. Who are cops going to believe? A respected businessman and player in Democratic Party politics or some gay hustler or a runaway?

'Rignall felt very much that he was dismissed by the police because of the attitudes at the time towards homosexuality,' executive producer of the Gacy documentary Alexa Danner later said. 'It's really hard to look back on that time today and understand how that could happen. It was a different time, but it caused a lot of suffering for that particular victim.'

' ... Yes, Gacy's name was mentioned in a few reports,' Albrecht said. 'And I guess you didn't have the interaction like you do now. Another process that came out of the Gacy case was much more contact and interaction between police departments.' He recalled that when Gacy finally hit his department's radar, they did an immediate background check on the man in question. 'Gacy was very well known in this community. When we went into bars and restaurants – a couple of times we went to a party that was going on – people just gravitated towards Gacy. He was very well liked,' Albrecht said. 'People were glad to see him. That continued during the time we were watching him [after he became a murder suspect], except that as it went on, many of these people were interviewed by other investigators about Gacy. And I think they started realising there was something going on here and started drifting away from him. And by the time the ten days of investigation were over, Gacy didn't have anybody really to talk to except us.'

Cops had another problem. Many of the young men and boys Gacy would murder were runaways and some of them were gay. Some were even tossed out of their homes and onto the mean streets of Chicago *because* of their sexual orientation. These kind of young men regularly went missing.

Serial killers like Samuel Little – who committed an estimated ninety-three murders over a two-decade stretch – are murderers of opportunity. But Little was also selective, kind of like a homicide sommelier. His victims were not the 'girls next door', professionals or Sue from the secretarial pool. They were women who lived life on the margins, often poor, drug-addicted and involved in sex work. They had been sucked into the anonymous underbelly of America. If no one knows – or cares – that you're missing, no one is going to report your disappearance. And if your name is not in the system, how are cops even going to know who you are?

A similar accusation was hurled at the Toronto Police Service in 2019 when it was revealed that, over a period of years, serial killer Bruce McArthur had preyed on gay men of colour. By the time he was arrested the landscaper and former sock salesman had murdered and dismembered ten men, leaving their remains scattered in the planters of his well-heeled gardening clients. Of course, they could have busted the serial killer much earlier but were accused of turning a blind eye to the horror unfolding before them because of the sexual orientation of the victims.

University of Western Ontario criminology professor and former cop Michael Arntfield said some of the people who fell into the clutches of Gacy, Little and McArthur are the 'missing missing'. 'Not to sound crude, but they [some of the victims] are an endangered species and it's incumbent upon society and the police to keep an eye out for people who are living on the margins,' Arntfield said at the height of the McArthur probe. 'If cops can get ahead of this, that will go a long way to cut down on murders and help them catch serial killers.' It's worth noting that, like Gacy, McArthur erected a façade of normalcy, even working as a shopping-mall Santa Claus.

Retired Des Plaines detective Michael Albrecht insisted to *Esquire* magazine in 2020, that the sexuality of some of the victims had nothing to do with Gacy's terrifyingly long run of murder. 'No, I don't think so at all. Of course it's much more accepted today as somebody's choice to make, and there's no issues with it,' he said of some of the victims' orientation. 'And back in the seventies, it wasn't like that.' But the retired detective again points out that there was a credibility gap between a gay hustler and a respected businessman. Four decades ago, it was almost always the latter that would be believed.

'One victim that Gacy had let go had tried to report him to the police and they looked at him a little bit, but not as much,' Albrecht said. 'I'm sure some of these detectives in Chicago might have followed up in instances where he let victims go, and Gacy would tell them, "Yeah, we had sexual contact and stuff like that but it wasn't forced in any way. It was consensual." And then he'd say how all of a sudden they're coming back to try to blackmail him because he's a successful businessman and all this kind of stuff.

'Gacy was a popular person. And then when we got involved with it, I mean, it [the homosexuality of some of the victims] certainly was never an issue. And Gacy did not like to be referred to as homosexual. He constantly told us he was not homosexual. He was bisexual at times, but not homosexual.'

As the 1970s were staggering to their dreary conclusion, Gacy was getting sloppy. After years of getting away with murder, he had become too confident and careless. And now he was out of storage space in the do-it-yourself crypt he had constructed under his suburban home. He buried two bodies in his backyard and then he began disposing of his prey in the rivers around Chicago where they would be discovered by police. That left him out in the open and gave detectives something to work with, although by late 1978 they were still not on to Gacy. Nor did they anticipate the magnitude of the slaughter which had been taking place right under their noses. The clock was ticking for John Wayne Gacy and 1978 would prove a fateful year. It wasn't the end for the well-connected contractor but you could see it in the distance.

4

The Nifty Fifties

The young John Wayne Gacy toughened up as he got older. The steady flow of slings and arrows fired by his brutish father were losing the impact they had once had. But they still stung – and they stung deeply.

His younger sister Karen told Oprah Winfrey in 2014 that growing up, she and her brother were best friends. Johnny did not have the same interests as his hard-bitten dad whose boozing had continued unabated. John Stanley liked fixing things and tooling around the house. John Wayne enjoyed gardening, baking and cooking. These were pastimes that John Stanley Gacy believed with all his heart were meant for women, not men – and certainly not the men of the Gacy household. It was not what the First World War veteran expected of his only son. The barrage of contempt for Johnny from his father was unyielding.

'My father, on many occasions, would call John a sissy. And he wasn't a happy drunk – sometimes he would turn into a mean drunk, so we had to always be real careful,' Karen said. 'John felt like he never lived up to Dad's expectations, and this went all the way into his adulthood, until he married and had a son and daughter.'

By the fifties, America was changing and so was Gacy's corner of it. Men wore their hair short and dressed neatly. The girls wore bobby sox. In the new, confident post-war America, an invention called television left the nation enthralled with Westerns like *Gunsmoke*, variety shows like *The Ed Sullivan Show* and comedies like *I Love Lucy*. On the radio, rock 'n' roll was replacing crooners like Perry Como as the soundtrack of the youth. It was still a buttoned-down, strait-laced world and the one that John Wayne Gacy grew up in.

Barry Boschelli became friends with the future killer at Cooley High in Chicago and in his book, *Johnny and Me: The True Story of John Wayne Gacy*, he offers considerable insight into Gacy.

'He was short, and his hair was slicked back. His shoes were scuffed. "What is your name?" I asked. He looked at me and said, "My name is John … Wayne … Gacy." We shook hands. Right at that moment, sir, there's no doubt, I knew that he was different from anyone that I ever knew,' Boschelli writes. 'I looked into his eyes when we were kids, and I saw sadness.'

Gacy is now known for his horrific crimes, his frequently bizarre art and his dual community roles of Pogo and Patches the Clown. It wasn't always that way, Boschelli said.

'What a lot of people don't know about Johnny … was that he was an extremely talented singer. It was Christmastime in the 1950s, and we'd go trudging through the snow. Our neighbours would invite us in, and I'd say, "Ladies and gentlemen, John Wayne Gacy will now sing 'O Holy Night'." When he poured it out, I can't tell you the effect that it had. I was there. I was lucky to be there. People would cry. He really touched and affected them,' Boschelli said years later.

Yes, Boschelli said, Gacy could have had a career in the showbiz world but standing in the way was his friend's troubled relationship with his dad. Besides singing, the two teenagers shared fraught relationships with their fathers. Boschelli's father was well connected with the Chicago political machine whose tentacles stretched across the country.

'My father knew a lot of people downtown at the time. He was very politically active with the mayor and could have easily helped Johnny get into show business. But I didn't get along with my dad so I couldn't ask him for favours,' Boschelli explained. 'If I could have, though, one of my favours would have been, "Dad, could you get Johnny into show business and get him to where he has to go?" I've always told myself this, and maybe I shouldn't hurt myself this way; I'm sorry, that's one of my regrets. Even if my father would have screamed and yelled at me, I should have pushed for it. At least I should have tried. Things could have ended up differently. Well, I didn't. I was scared of my father. Scared to death.'

After high school, the two boys went their separate ways. Boschelli was a year older and was going down a different path. For seventeen years, the two boys – who had now grown into men – lost contact, until one day in 1976. But the two squabbled and any hope of resuscitating the friendship was DOA. Two years later, the name John Wayne Gacy re-entered Boschelli's consciousness via screaming headlines and round-the-clock coverage on radio and television.

Boschelli was there when the infamous swing hit Gacy in the head. He notes that things changed. He became a different kid.

'I can't … it's just hard [to reconcile the fact Gacy was a serial killer]. I knew him when he was eight years old. These actions were not in him then. He just wasn't capable of it. One day when we were hanging out a few years later, a swing accidentally knocked him across the forehead. He fell to the ground unconscious. Fifteen or twenty of us had to carry him home in a wagon. I didn't see him again for about a week. When I finally did, he was different. He was not the same no more. He was very nervous – he'd be snapping his fingers all the time, it just wasn't the same any more. I knew then things are starting to change now.'

By his teenage years, Gacy was increasingly worried about his health. He would be considered on the verge of being a hypochondriac. The fainting spells that plagued him since the head injury continued.

As for girls, he could take them or leave them. For a while during these years he even considered entering the priesthood. For his devout Catholic father, this was something that might at last have made him happy and maybe dispelled John Stanley Gacy's deeply held view that his son was a 'sissy'. But Gacy later admitted that sometimes late in the evenings in his bedroom by himself, he thought of embracing one of his friends – one of his male friends.

He seemed to sense that his stern father knew what he was thinking – and he didn't like it. Living with his father – his moods, his archaic worldview and his overflowing cup of bitterness – could turn the heartiest of souls into a nervous wreck. When he was twenty years old, in 1962, John Wayne Gacy had had enough of his father's stifling discipline and demeaning comments. In spite of John Stanley Gacy's unrelenting cruelty, his son was moving on.

In the manuscript he turned over to *The New Yorker* and other publications, Gacy discusses leaving home at length (it has been edited here for clarity):

In the first three months of 1962, I hadn't been working and I had my dad on my back about everything. There wasn't nothing I could do that was right to him. I had to pay him $100 a month as part of the money he put up so that I could get a car and by March I had fallen one payment behind. By April, he was threatening to take away the car, so on the 6 or 9 of April, I decided to run away. I knew I had a cousin out west; the last known place where she lived was Las Vegas. She was a high-priced hooker, not married but with a child. She had run away from home two years before me. Uncle Ray made an attempt to talk her into coming back by making a trip out there, but she refused, since she enjoyed what she was doing and had a home of her own, with a maid. She became the black sheep of the family.

In any case, I watched enough TV to know that Route 66 went out west, and that's all I had going for me when I left. One morning after everyone was gone from the house, I loaded the car with the personal things that I was going to take with me. Then the phone rang – mother was calling to ask me to pick her up from work at noon, as she wasn't feeling well. I went out to Dor-O-Matic and brought her home, dropped her off and told her I was going to get the car gassed up.

Then I just left. Irving Park to the tollway, then south to Route 66, towards Springfield, Illinois. That first evening I got as far as 100 miles north of St Louis. I pulled over to the rest area and slept in the car. The next morning, I took off across the rest of Illinois, all of Missouri, stopping to see some caves on the way, then the south-east corner of Kansas and into Oklahoma, where I spent the night in a motel.

I had to watch my money, as I left home with $136.00, all I had to my name. The next morning west out of Oklahoma City, down 66 across Texas, upper part, to New Mexico. I stopped for the night in Albuquerque, again sleeping in a motel. Then across the rest of New Mexico, into Arizona, through Kingman, and on to Nevada. By late afternoon I hit the Hoover Dam and was in time to go on the last tour of the day. After that, Las Vegas. It's a great sight to see all those lights coming in from off the plains. There were so many motels. I couldn't believe it.

Fabulous Las Vegas found the young John Wayne Gacy, tired and disoriented and uncertain about what his future would hold in his shocking new surroundings.

I was so tired from the driving all I could think of was finding a place to shower and go to bed. I paid for one night at a place, and it left me just a little more than $35.00. I woke around noon, checked out, and went sightseeing, ending up in a downtown casino. Whereby, I went through $25.00 with no luck on my side. In three short hours, I had gone through two-thirds of all I had. I walked to my car, which was parked in the sun. Of course, coming from Chicago, I had the windows up and no way for the air to get out. I had a lot on my mind, wondering what I was going to do next, where could I get more money, wondering what was going on at home, since this was the first time I had thought of my family since leaving three days before.

I got in the car, closed the door, and just sat there with the windows up; the heat got to me so fast I didn't know that I had passed out. The next thing I remember was a police officer pulling me out of the car, and hearing an ambulance coming up the street. I kept saying that I was all right, but he said that I had to go to the hospital (another expense I did not need). I told the doctors I didn't have any money, couldn't afford it, but they said the county would pay their bill. The ambulance ride cost $34.00 and wasn't covered. I got back to my car around ten that night, had about $7.00 to my name, so drove north out to the desert, pulled off the road, and [was] sleeping in the car again.

Oddly, the young Chicagoan found work that suited him.

Next morning I stopped in a gas station and, after cleaning up in the restroom, got a city map, as I wanted to know where the ambulance company was. I had decided I would just go and be honest, telling the owner I would work it off, had no money. I went into the office and told him my problem and that I would wash his ambulances, or anything else he wanted to pay the bill. He said that he liked my honesty and wondered if I would want a steady job. I told him I would, but had no place to stay. He said I could grab one of the bunks in the ambulance room. I agreed and had a job.

The first day off I got, I found my cousin's name in the phone book and went looking for her. The third time I went to her house, I happened to pull up just as she was going into her driveway. She was surprised to see me and asked me in. She talked honest and frank about her business in front of the maid and her little girl. She talked about the money, $200 a trick, and wondered if I was offended by what she was doing. I told her, hell it was her body and I guess she could do what she wanted. She had a new home, new Cadillac convertible, a maid full time, and she would get up at noon and have breakfast. It was a new enlightenment to me, so open about sexual conversation, as if nothing was wrong with anything. She worshipped the child and wanted the best of everything for her, and by the way she was living was doing all right. I would meet many of her friends, and she said that she would fix me up with any of them I wanted, meaning sexually, but I turned her down. I told her I would find my own. I felt funny doing that with her knowing.

After working nearly two months, I was told that I would have to get a work card, since the ambulance company had city contracts. In order to get a work card in Las Vegas you have to be twenty-one, I was not. The owner said that he thought he had a job for me at a mortuary, being their night man and picking up remains from the hospital and sometimes from the homes.

Again I was able to live right there. The room where I stayed was known as the call room, right next to the embalming room. During May the mortuary had eighty-six funerals and over two months I was pallbearer for some seventy-five, never knowing the person or family.

Gacy's new digs were in the morgue. Gacy later told *The New Yorker* that one night in the mortuary he climbed into the coffin of a boy who had died. The enterprising future serial killer arranged the body on top of him. The corpse strangely left the young Gacy with an erection.

That taste of the forbidden terrified Gacy, and after a few months in Las Vegas he had grown homesick for Chicago and his family. The next day he called his mother. He wanted to come home to Chicago. Would it be all right with his father?

In the summer of 1962, John Wayne Gacy returned to his hometown, determined to make his father proud and become a success. Initially, he enrolled at a community college where he took business courses.

The next entry on the Gacy CV was a job selling shoes. Sales was something the personable young man was well suited to do. He did so well that his employer transferred him to Illinois's capital, Springfield, about three hours south of Chicago, but a million miles away culturally. Quiet and staid it was a world away from his raucous hometown. But the job was a big promotion with Gacy overseeing sales of the company's shoes in a large department store. And he brought that old Chicago hustle to the task at hand, trading shoes for fine clothes with salesmen who visited.

'The Jockey man would come in and get a pair of $40 shoes at cost,' Gacy wrote in one letter to writer Alec Wilkinson. 'I would get a dozen briefs and Jockey T-shirts, sometimes more. It was the same with shirts, nothing but the best. Manhattan French-cuff white shirts, some silk, some of the finest cotton Van Heusen shirts the same way – shoes for shirts … You talk about men's jewellery, hell again I had the best of Swank cufflinks, tie-pins. I had a collection of stones of the world in cuff-links. I liked large flashy cuff-links, as women would always remark about my dress.'

He added, 'Psychologically, I got recognition from the customers, always remarking about my cufflinks, or ties, and never the same. I enjoyed the attention … and it made a good impression on the customer, not only would they know I was the manager, but just by looking at me, you knew I had to be the boss … I dressed and looked like an owner or a millionaire even when I was young …'

Gacy also followed some fashion rules and advice from old pros.

'I never wore brown because a man from Hart Schaffner Marx said I didn't look good in brown … I liked rich dark blues, blacks, burgundy, greys, olives; some wool, but I stayed with sharkskins and silks because of the richness.'

And Gacy also discovered he was a masterful fundraiser. He even organised a charity show that featured an up-and-coming band riding the crest of the wave of British Invasion acts: The Kinks, performers of radio-friendly hits like 'Lola', 'Till the End of the Day' and scores of others.

In Springfield, Gacy lived with his aunt and uncle. He had also caught the eye of a young sales girl who worked for him.

Her name was Marlynn Myers, the daughter of a wealthy businessman. It was a whirlwind romance and the couple would marry in September 1964.

But Gacy's inner narrative was developing what would be buried in the depths of his troubled soul for years – a chilling story arc. About the time he got hitched, Gacy also had his first homosexual encounter. While boozing at a buddy's house, Gacy had imbibed too much and passed out. When he awoke, he was shocked to find his penis in his friend's mouth. At the time, the young businessman felt he couldn't tell the guy to stop. In addition, Gacy would later admit that he enjoyed the experience. However, he also admitted that for months afterwards, any thoughts of the encounter repulsed and depressed him.

No doubt the ominous spectre of his violent and stern father hung over the incident. It would not be something John Stanley would ever approve of. Years later, Gacy's mother Marion said that if her late husband knew that their son had sex with men 'he would have killed him.'

His sister Karen agreed that their father was a cruel brute, unfit to raise a gnat, let alone a child. But she drew the line at blaming John Stanley Gacy for turning her brother into a monster.

'I don't know what I feel guilty about. He was my brother; he did it. They weren't my choices,' Karen told Oprah Winfrey.

'I don't want other people that have even a son or a daughter that do something, I don't want them to think that they're a bad parent. People have choices after they're a certain age, and if they make the right choices, their life is good. But if they make the wrong choices, it's not, and I've worked with people in prison, and that was where I got a lot of my healing from.'

There was an unbearable amount of pain to come for the Gacy family and anyone else who came into contact with John Wayne Gacy. But the 1960s were ready to swing, and so was Gacy.

5

The Swinging Sixties

John Stanley Gacy had to admit that maybe he had been wrong about his son. Maybe he had been too harsh on the boy when he was a child. The old First World War veteran's change of heart was no doubt spurred on by the marriage of his only son, John Wayne Gacy, to the lovely Marlynn Myers. For the old man, it finally dispelled the notion that John Wayne may have been a 'sissy'.

John Stanley Gacy – now sixty-four – was watching as the world was changing. His son had enjoyed a meteoric rise at the shoe company, and had been promoted to management within three weeks. He still believed his son was a 'patsy' for supporting the Democratic Party over his favoured Republicans, but the boy had settled down, married and was fast becoming a success in the booming America of the early sixties. In Springfield, his son had even become involved with the popular service club, the Jaycees, one of many that thrived in the post-war years. It was ideal for networking, meeting new people and burnishing one's people skills. He was clearly a young man on the move.

Fred Myers, Marlynn's dad, didn't like Gacy, but he was more than willing to give his daughter and only child the best possible start in life. And if that included John Wayne Gacy, then so be it. In 1966, the young man was offered the opportunity of a lifetime, courtesy of Fred Myers. His father-in-law had purchased three Kentucky Fried Chicken restaurants in Waterloo, Iowa, about 305 miles north-west of Springfield. These were the years before fast-food chains were as ubiquitous as they are today, but business at KFC was booming. Fred needed a manager and wanted Gacy to take the reins. Myers would provide the couple with a home and pay his son-in-law $15,000 plus a 20% bonus on the profits. That's about $130,000 base salary in 2022 dollars. It was the deal of a lifetime.

Marlynn quickly fell pregnant with the couple's first child. After completing a management course at Kentucky Fried Chicken University in Louisville, Kentucky John joined his wife in Waterloo. Gacy would later describe his life in the mid-sixties as 'perfect'.

Waterloo was not exactly the Pleasantville it might have seemed to be at first glance. It had a population of around 70,000 people and its packing houses and factories were booming. But Waterloo's large Black community had long resented their second-class status and in the mid-sixties in turmoil-racked America, that resentment exploded into riots.

Still, for a young white businessman like John Wayne Gacy it seemed like a great place to raise a young family. Gacy joined the Waterloo chapter of the Jaycees. And the Jaycees in Waterloo loved Gacy – he was hard-working, affable and always ready to lend a hand or donate a few buckets of chicken if needed. Gacy worked very hard, often ten to fourteen hours a day. But, as important as his career was to him, the Jaycees were more important. Up to fifty events were held each year by the organisation and Gacy was invariably involved in the organising of every one. But while he was liked and respected for his devotion to the club, not everyone was buying the mover-and-shaker act.

'He had a hell of a big-man complex,' former Jaycee Steve Pottinger told writer Tim Cahill, author of *Buried Dreams: Inside the Mind of a Serial Killer*, adding that others found the Chicago native an overbearing loudmouth. And Gacy began insisting fellow members, his employees at the restaurants and other friends call him 'The Colonel' after Colonel Harland Sanders, the founder of the Kentucky Fried Chicken empire.

'John was a heck of a promoter,' his friend Charles Hill recalled. 'And I would say you could classify him as a great con artist. He had a lot of con about him; he could manipulate people and get them to do things, both for the Jaycees and himself, too … The club was his whole life.' Once, the club was short of members and, in an afternoon, Gacy went out and recruited twenty more men to join their merry band. Gacy's skills of persuasion were helped by the fact that one of his key recruitment methods was to hold parties with free booze and screenings of pornographic 'stag' films. Gacy would also employ sex workers for these events. He received a pin from the Jaycees after signing sixty new members in 1967.

The Colonel was making boffo bucks and he was also a rising star in the Jaycees where, by 1967, he had been appointed to their board of directors. That Summer of Love year, Gacy also began overseeing the club's religious affairs as the chapter's so-called 'chaplain'.

But Gacy was a bullshitter and anyone who knew him could see it. Not happy that his friends simply called him The Colonel because of his KFC affiliation, he was now insisting that he was a *real* colonel and had served with distinction in the United States Marine Corps. Then, he changed tack and said his title came from something called the Governor's Brigade of Illinois, his home state. Of course, years later, Gacy still insisted he was a colonel – a Kentucky colonel. But that's not a real honour. Anyone can get a certificate declaring that the bearer is a Kentucky Colonel through the mail; all you have to do is ask.

In the wider societal background of the turbulent sixties, sexual mores were rapidly changing. Some of the younger Jaycees were reportedly not above a little wife-swapping and held the odd swingers' party on occasion. And booze? It flowed like the Mississippi.

Once when Gacy and Marlynn were having dinner with Hill and his wife, 'The Colonel' hinted that maybe his friend might like to have sex with his unsuspecting wife. Gacy's lurid offer was rebuffed and he later acted as though it was all a gag. Hill wasn't so sure.

Since he had been a child, Gacy had always been fascinated by cops and police work. In Waterloo, he jumped at an opportunity to join a Keystone Kops-like organisation called the Merchant Patrol. It was a volunteer organisation that kept an eye on local businesses as a way to take the pressure off police. Gacy relished his new role and even carried a gun and had a flashing red light that he kept in his car. It was a chilling harbinger of what was to come. But, at the time, Gacy, the braggart and a show-off, loved using the red light to get a little attention. It was all a bit of a giggle, really. Whilst attending a Jaycees' convention in Phoenix, Charley Hill, Jaycee president was running late for a meeting. 'Charley told me, "Goddamn it, I got business, I gotta be there!",' Gacy later told Tim Cahill. The Colonel knew how to get him where he was going, pronto. 'So I take him and reach under the seat for the red light we used on the Merchant Patrol, just lean out the window and put the light on the hood. Then I pulled out, around all the traffic, crossed the double yellow line, and took off like a bat. Lights flashing, the whole works. Went right through every intersection.' The two men arrived two minutes early for Hill's appointment.

Gacy was also known to deliver free fried chicken to police precincts in Waterloo as a goodwill gesture – and maybe to finagle a future get-out-of-jail-free card – one that he could use if he was caught driving drunk or was found holding a stag night with porn films and sex workers.

His father-in-law didn't approve of The Colonel wasting money by giving away chicken to the cops. Gacy still wasn't winning over his father-in-law. Peter could never really put his finger on it, but there was something that rubbed him the wrong way about his son-in-law. What he didn't know – could not have known – was that Gacy was involved in some less than wholesome side activities. For his part, Gacy felt Fred Myers was increasingly becoming more like his own father: never happy, always complaining.

Nevertheless, in 1967 things were going very well for Gacy. He and Marlynn had welcomed their baby boy in 1966 and a daughter followed in 1967. He was a respected business and family man, a pillar of the community and had built a solid façade of the perfect Midwestern American family.

The family lived in a tidy bungalow on Fairlane Street in Waterloo and, like his father before him, Gacy spent hours in his workshop. He was forever making home improvements whether it was the driveway, the garden or the house itself. Gacy appeared to love his children, taking them with him on his rounds of the KFC outlets and on Jaycees' business at the Clayton House Hotel.

During this blissful time, there was even a detente of sorts with his father. It had been a long time coming. On a visit from Chicago by his father, they cruised the streets of Waterloo in The Colonel's new Oldsmobile Vista Cruiser, talking as a man and his father should. After seeing the perfect life his son had built for himself, John Stanley offered his hand and told John Wayne, 'I was wrong about you, John.'

It may have been the single most gratifying moment of Gacy's life. Since he was a child all he had ever wanted was the love and approval of his father, who had dismissed and ridiculed everything his son had ever done. And now, Gacy had that desperately needed validation from the most important man in his world.

The Jaycees didn't just offer an outlet for professional advancement, they offered political opportunities for an ambitious young man like the beefy Chicagoan. Gacy later told Tim Cahill that he was seriously considering a possible political career during those years.

'Back then,' Gacy said, 'I was thinking of running for alderman. After that I wanted to go for mayor, and if that worked, I was going to run for the state senate. I didn't see any limits.'

By July 1967, Gacy had been named 'Outstanding Vice-President' of the local Jaycees chapter as well as maintaining his post as chapter chaplain and general chairman of the first city-wide prayer breakfast slated for that November. The window-dressing was perfect and Gacy's dark secrets remained hidden, his perversions were still locked away in the black recesses of his mind and soul.

'Nobody had the idea that John Gacy would turn out to be the monster that he did,' Gacy's former lawyer, Al Frerichs, told the *Waterloo Courier* in 1994. Later, and for decades afterwards, people who knew Gacy in Waterloo tried to ascertain what it all meant. What had they missed? Was there something about Gacy that they should have spotted?

To give the good burghers of Waterloo a pass, no one knew back then there were men like John Wayne Gacy. At the time, middle America was largely unaware that there were evil, twisted men lurking in plain sight in their pristine small towns. And if there was an acknowledgement that people like that existed, their predilections would be brushed off or go completely under the radar. They'd be described as 'funny' – but not 'funny, ha, ha' – you know, 'funny'. Parents who had some awareness would caution their children to avoid certain men.

But some people who knew The Colonel suspected something was off about him – something not quite right. There were young men who worked for him (and they were almost all teenage boys) and neighbours who, quite frankly, he creeped out.

Joe Sink worked for Gacy at one of the KFC outlets when he was a teenager. Sink later said that Gacy was 'always acting like a big shot', adding that he didn't like him and 'regardless of my age at the time, I could see he was a jerk.'

Former neighbour Bill Fulton added, 'He had some of the kids who were working for him going in and out of the house all the time.' He had opened something of a club in the basement of his home, and he would invite the boys who worked for him over to drink booze, play pool and watch porn. He only ever socialised with his male employees; there was an unspoken no-girls-allowed policy with The Colonel. Sometimes, he would make sexual overtures to these teenagers and, if these clumsy efforts were spurned, Gacy would claim it was just a joke.

However, many of his friends in the Jaycees didn't see this side of Gacy. Gacy was a natural-born salesman who was 'a very hard-working individual'. Outwardly he appeared every inch the successful family man.

At Christmas, Gacy and his pal Charley Hill were each paired with two kids for a shopping spree as part of a Jaycees' event. Each child was given $5 to spend on presents. Gacy walked hand in hand with the two kids he had been assigned.

'One of the children John was with ran out of money and started crying,' Hill later recalled. 'John pulled money out of his pocket and gave it to him.'

So, on the one hand, there was John Wayne Gacy: champion of children, and on the other hand there was someone completely different. There was the John Wayne Gacy who indulged in wife-swapping and, hired sex workers for porn-fuelled parties with young men. At just twenty-six, he was already leading a tortured double life. But the clock was ticking for John Wayne Gacy. And it struck midnight on the evening of 10 May 1968. Detectives knocked on the door of his pleasant home, on a pleasant street, in a pleasant Midwestern town and arrested him. The crime was sodomy.

The alleged incident had occurred the previous August. The boy's name was Donald Voorhees and his father was a fellow Jaycee and a friend of Gacy. Donald was just fifteen years old. Marlynn had taken the children to visit friends in Illinois and Gacy had the house to himself. Gacy invited the boy inside for some refreshments.

Gacy later told author Tim Cahill his account of the incident. He was driving in his car on the evening in question when he heard a boy yelling, 'Hey, Mr Gacy!' He said he had immediately recognised Donald Voorhees Jr., the handsome, muscular son of his Jaycees pal. His father had confided in The Colonel that there had recently been trouble at home and that father and son were not getting along.

Gacy said he asked the boy, 'How are you getting along with your old man these days?'

Donald Jr. said things were 'all right' but didn't elaborate.

Remembering his own dark days dealing with his father, Gacy knew where the teen was coming from. Gacy persisted, 'You ever think your dad might have a point here? You ever stop to look at it from his side? My dad – we never got along when I was your age. I could never do anything right. Even ran away from home, but that's not the way you solve anything. We get along okay now, and I see where he gave me my drive and shit.

If I didn't have drive, I wouldn't have my degree in accounting and my degree in business administration. I wouldn't have a nice house. Wouldn't own three restaurants. It's part of growing up, feeling that way about your dad, I think. Then, later on, you see it from another perspective.'

The boy was nonplussed. 'I suppose,' he said.

Gacy didn't like the snarly teen's response. He said, 'So what the hell are you doing here anyway?'

The boy responded, 'I was at my girlfriend's house, I was walking home. I don't get my licence until next year.'

Gacy then asked the boy if he had ever been laid. The conversation moved to stag films and The Colonel later claimed it was the kid who brought up the subject. His dad had told him about some of the Jaycees' parties. He told the young man that he had some films back at his house.

Today, pornography is ubiquitous. At the push of a computer button there is enough filth to keep a teen boy erect until graduation in whatever variation he might desire. But in the sixties, porn was still a dirty secret reserved just for Jaycees, Shriners and other men's clubs. The stuff had to be ordered through the mail or purchased in a brown paper bag. Hardcore porn was difficult to find and it was very, very expensive. If you were caught with it, a hefty fine and even jail time could potentially be in the offing. So when Gacy said he suggested that maybe young Voorhees should come back to his house, kick back and watch some loops it would have been difficult for a young teenage boy to resist.

Later, Gacy would insist to Cahill that this offer was made strictly out of the goodness of his heart. Nothing up his sleeve, honest. He told the teen, 'You're getting to an age where you can get a good educational experience out of something like that.'

Gacy said he set up the projector and let the boy watch the action unfold while he grabbed a beer and a sandwich. During an oral-sex scene in which a woman was performing fellatio on a man, Gacy dug into his well of bullshit to seal the deal.

The controversial Kinsey Report had been published at the end of the fifties. Among other findings it claimed that almost half of the male subjects examined had reacted sexually to people of both sexes and that at least 37% had had at least one homosexual experience.

'The thing of it is,' The Colonel began, 'read the Kinsey Report and it shows how most guys your age sometimes go down on a guy. Or have a guy go down on them. It don't mean you're a queer; it's part of growing up, becoming a man. Nobody tells you this shit, but ... but it's scientific, and you could read it in the reports ... You have to have sex with a man before you start having sex with women,' Gacy told the boy. Gacy later told Cahill he almost believed his own bullshit. Gacy now had his hooks in the boy who would become his first victim. But who would go down on who first? 'There's nothing wrong with anything,' Gacy told young Voorhees. 'Unless you make it wrong in your own mind.'

Gacy decided he would go first. The kid ejaculated but Gacy noticed the young Donald's hands were shaking. He told Donald Voorhees Jr. it was all just like 'sucking on your thumb'. Then Gacy recalled – would you believe it? – the kid stuck his thumb in his mouth! Gacy admitted that it was all he could do to keep himself from laughing out loud at the boy he had just sexually assaulted. He gave Voorhees $50 to keep his mouth shut.

According to Gacy, Voorhees kept coming back, asking for more cash. He believed he was being blackmailed. At least that's what he told people – and probably himself too.

'Each time,' Gacy told Cahill, 'I thought, well, I'll just give him a little more money, help him get straightened out, and that'll be the last time I see him.' For months, Voorhees kept his mouth shut about what was happening with Gacy. Gacy later said he knew this was all becoming a big problem for him. In the shadows of the well-ordered life he presented to the world, a tidal wave of turmoil was raging. It was a big problem for the boy he had groomed and victimised too. Donald was feeling a crushing amount of guilt and revulsion. John Wayne Gacy was terrified his secrets would get out and destroy everything he had built and carrying that secret around was a tortured young man.

Eventually, Voorhees couldn't keep it to himself anymore and finally, in March 1968, turned to his father and told him what had happened with Gacy. His dad called the cops.

The dark path John Wayne Gacy had been treading alongside his public life was in danger of being revealed to the world. But he wasn't ready to let events roll over him like a steamroller. He would fight back.

6

Gacy's Waterloo

In late 1967, John Wayne Gacy had a problem that threatened to ruin everything. His father-in-law Fred Myers wasn't going to allow him to continue to oversee the KFC empire in Waterloo, Iowa, if he knew what Gacy had been up to behind the doors at Fairlane Street. He would also lose his wife, Marlynn, his two children, his membership of the Jaycees and a shot at a political career. Was he willing to let that happen? Forget it. No, this kid was a serious problem.

Gacy had continued to pay fifteen-year-old Donald Voorhees for sex. Now, the kid wanted more money. Gacy later claimed that he realised he was being blackmailed. It's unclear whether Gacy thought that Voorhees was a willing participant. 'Let's just say he did what he did. Whether he was really into it would just be supposition on my part,' Gacy later told Tim Cahill. 'But he kept coming back, and whether it was for the money or the sex, I'd have to conclude that it was a willing thing on his part.' Either way, no matter how you cut it, Donald was a minor and it was illegal. Gacy could victim-blame as much as he wanted but what he was doing with a young boy was both criminal and morally abhorrent.

Gacy was also starting to resent how much money he was shelling out to the kid and began to feel he was being 'fucked over'. And, he told Cahill, that – worst of all – he felt that the teenager was outsmarting him. He told Cahill about an incident during the Christmas holidays in 1967, Voorhees came knocking on Gacy's door once again. The kid was in a band and he wanted to 'borrow' money from Gacy for a new amplifier, or at least that's the way he told it. He and his bandmates were slated to play a New Year's Eve bash.

He allegedly told Gacy: 'My dad won't lend me the money, so I thought maybe you could.' The amp was maybe $100. The kid told Gacy he would for sure pay him back. Gacy later said the two reached a compromise and he fronted the kid enough money to rent a decent amp. He didn't even want payback.

'I thought he could [use the amp] to keep making money and that he wouldn't come to me for it any more. I told him, "This is the last time. I don't want to see you around here anymore … You think you can tell about us, but I'll just deny everything. Who do you think they're going to believe? Asshole!" And that was the last I heard of Voorhees until May of the next year.'

No doubt Gacy let out a sigh of relief when the kid stopped coming around. What he could not have known was that young Donald Voorhees Jr. would eventually confess everything to his father in March 1968. And in a lot of ways, Gacy had a con artist's confidence, thinking 'I'm going to get away with this.' It never really occurred to him that he could lose everything.

There had been lurid little whispers around Waterloo about Gacy's appreciation for young men. The Colonel had a thing for boys, the story went. There were others who scoffed at the idea. But … there always seemed to be teenage boys around Gacy – both at the KFC restaurants he managed and also at his home. When Voorhees told his father what had been happening in March 1968, people who knew Gacy were shocked. He would tell anyone who would listen that it was *him* who was really the victim here. He had been naive, gullible ... the boy was blackmailing him.

However, it wasn't just Donald Voorhees Jr. who had fallen victim to John Wayne Gacy. There was another kid with a horrifying story to tell, named Mark Miller. And the story Miller told was a chilling foreshadowing of what was to come a decade later in suburban Chicago.

Miller worked at one of Gacy's Kentucky Fried Chicken outlets. He cleaned the floors and sometimes he manned the deep fryer. After work one day in 1967, he said, Gacy offered to give him a lift home. The high-flying Jaycee had invited him to come into the house. Marlynn wasn't home. In fact, she was in the hospital giving birth to the couple's daughter. It would just be the guys. So Gacy served the kid some whiskey and they watched some dirty movies ... and then Gacy attacked, choking the boy out until he nearly fell unconscious. And once Gacy had the boy restrained, he proceeded to rape him. Violently.

When the kid woke up from his nightmare Gacy was apologetic. Sorry about that. No harm done. He gave Miller a ride home then fired him several days later.

A year later, the rumours about Gacy were becoming truths. He was indicted in May 1968 by a Black Hawk County grand jury for committing the act of sodomy on a teenage boy for his attack on Miller.

Ever the scam artist, Gacy denied everything. No, Miller had had *willing* sexual relations with him – for money. It was, Gacy would later tell the court, part of an elaborate sting by Jaycee members who didn't want him to be president of the local chapter. Once Voorhees and Miller came forward, more boys began coming forward with stories about the odd Mr. Gacy. One was even lured with the promise of sex with Marlynn and once the hook was set, the boy was blackmailed into performing oral sex on Gacy. Other teens were recruited into his sick scheme with the promise of $50 each. The KFC big wheel even used the Kinsey Report to claim he had been commissioned to conduct homosexual experiments for the purpose of scientific research. Gacy had been sexually abusing other boys.

The carefully constructed veneer of respectability around John Wayne Gacy had begun to wear thin. Of course there had been rumours that Gacy had homosexual inclinations. But that veneer now started to crack. These were young boys that had been abused and raped.

'It was breaking that quickly that we were getting stories from each of the young people we interviewed,' former Black Hawk County Assistant District Attorney Dave Dutton told the *Waterloo Chronicle* in 1994. 'It finally came down to one boy [Miller] and he gave us enough to go on.'

Not content in his belief that a jury would be likely to believe a respected businessman over a teenage boy, The Colonel was leaving absolutely nothing to chance. Enter West High football hero, eighteen-year-old Dwight Andersson.

Gacy engaged the beefy Andersson to beat up Miller – give the boy a scare so he'd back off and change his mind about testifying. The deal was $10 plus $300 more down the road – more than enough to pay off Andersson's car loan. Gacy even gave the kid a can of mace to use on the little bigmouth. Andersson was told to warn Miller not to implicate Mr. Gacy with his 'sick lies'.

The jock even befriended Miller as the plan went into motion, with the younger boy becoming more comfortable with his new pal. Then, one day in September 1968, the two teenagers drove to a local forest where Andersson surprised Miller, spraying his 'friend's' face with mace before beating him. But things didn't go according to plan for the jock. Miller fought back and broke

Andersson's nose before running to safety and a nearby river where he washed the noxious chemical out of his eyes.

Miller then called the cops, who paid young Master Andersson a visit and took him into custody. The scared teenager told detectives that John Wayne Gacy had paid him to give Miller a beating. Gacy was arrested again – this time it was on charges of attempted perjury, going armed with intent and malicious threats to extort.

A Black Hawk County judge ordered that Gacy undergo psychiatric evaluation. Was this well-known businessman mentally competent to stand trial? In the end, he would be ruled fit. However, the 1968 psychological report on Gacy offers a startling insight into his mind and motivations. The report diagnosed Gacy as having an antisocial personality. And it confirmed that any sort of medical treatment or therapy would likely not do much good.

'The most striking aspect of the test results is the patient's total denial of responsibility for everything that has happened to him,' the report excerpt reads. 'He can produce an "alibi" for everything. He presents himself as a victim of circumstances and blames other people who are out to get him … the patient attempts to assure a sympathetic response by depicting himself as being at the mercy of a hostile environment.'

A Jaycees rival, Peter Burk was clear-eyed when discussing Gacy. 'He was not a man tempered by the truth. He seemed unaffected when caught in lies.'

Waterloo lawyer and fellow Jaycee Tom Langlas agreed. 'He was a glad-hander type who would go beyond that. He'd shower too much attention as a way of getting more attention himself.'

Gacy must have known his goose was cooked. Even from the few friends and cronies who stood by him and bizarrely believed in his innocence, he kept one secret close to his chest. He had demanded a lie-detector test in Black Hawk County and he had failed it. The joke among cops and prosecutors in Waterloo was that the only answer Gacy gave that was true was his name.

Still, he was a respectable businessman – he could wriggle out of this. Maybe he would get probation or a short county sentence. So, he pleaded guilty to the charge of sodomy (against Voorhees but not the other boys) in December 1968 and held his breath. The DA dropped perjury and other charges. Gacy expected to get a slap on the wrist. He was very, very wrong. Judge Peter Van Metre sentenced Gacy to ten years in the slammer, the maximum sentence. During sentencing, the judge told Gacy: 'For some period of time you cannot seek out teenage boys to solicit them for immoral behavior of any kind.' And that was that.

'I can't claim any great wisdom or anything, but somehow I just didn't think this guy should have been turned loose,' the amazingly prescient Van Metre said in a 1994 interview. 'He had already shown the signs ... he could have gone ahead and did what he did in Chicago.'

In retrospect, the Assistant District Attorney in charge of the prosecution, Dave Dutton, said that the sex attacks in Waterloo pointed to the future serial killer's ability to deceive people and get them to trust him. 'He would take some of the boys to his home after work in Waterloo,' Dutton told the hometown paper. 'While he was there, some of them were chained to the bed while he and others engaged in sexual activity in front of these children. He would threaten and beat the boys that didn't do what he wanted them to.' Both he and Metre recognised that the justice system ultimately failed and would tragically end up letting forty boys and young men down. But no one knew that at the time.

What was clear was that the carefully constructed environment John Wayne Gacy had created for himself – a disturbing duality of light and dark – had shattered into a million pieces.

While he sat for ninety days in the Black Hawk County jail, awaiting a transfer to the Iowa State Reformatory for Men to start his ten-year sentence, Gacy got more bad news. His long-suffering wife Marlynn was filing for divorce on the grounds he had violated their wedding vows. Gacy would never again see his children, Michael and Christine.

Marlynn Gacy divorced her husband on 18 September 1969. The grounds were cruel and inhumane treatment. There was no question over custody of the children. She eventually remarried and changed her name. Bringing up the name John Wayne Gacy sent shivers down her spine. And yet, when her ex-husband was arrested in 1978 for the horrors in Chicago, Marlynn told one reporter that the news stunned her. She had never seen it coming.

'I just couldn't believe it,' Marlynn said. 'I never had any fear of him. It's hard for me to relate to these killings. I was never afraid of him.'

His ex-wife was also in denial at the idea that her former husband had a penchant for men and boys. Marlynn would say she had 'problems believing that he was homosexual'. Nothing in their short married life had prepared her for that. She just didn't see it. John was never violent and he was great with their two kids. In an interview, conducted in the late 1970s, Marlynn circled back to her husband's father, John Stanley Gacy. If John Wayne had developed any mental problems they were no doubt the result of his father's cruelty.

'He and his dad did not get along. They were never close,' Marlynn said, without explaining the relationship one step further.

In March 1969, Gacy, then twenty-six years old, entered prison for the very first time. The prison was in Anamosa, Iowa, outside Cedar Rapids and, figuratively, about a million miles away from his hometown of Chicago. With a population of only around 4,000, according to the 1970 U. S. census, there was not much to see outside the four concrete walls that were to be Gacy's new abode. The maximum security prison was a grim old fortress, built in 1875 and holding around 1,000 violent criminals. This was a startling new experience for Gacy.

There was also the frightening reality that child sex offenders were on the lowest rung of the prison pecking order. Jailbirds would not hesitate to 'shank a paedo'. In fact, their status in the jungle that is prison would soar if they were to take out a kiddie-fiddler.

But Gacy – ever the conman – turned out to be a model prisoner. He obeyed the rules and kept his nose clean. Cons are nothing if not savvy on how to game the system. The former KFC supervisor knew that if he behaved himself, particularly in those days of prison reform and liberalisation, he could skate on out of there with early parole.

Back in Waterloo, the social circles Gacy moved in were still in shock. At the time, his Jaycees buddy Charley Hill still believed in Gacy's innocence. He often wrote letters to his imprisoned pal. Everyone else – apart from his family back in Chicago – 'dropped him like a hot potato' said Hill. Gacy still maintained that he was an innocent man in his responses to Hill. It was a 'set-up for political reasons' and he had been railroaded by the powers that be – the cops, the judge and the prosecution.

In prison, Gacy settled in displaying his old hustle and can-do attitude. He even set up a chapter of his beloved Jaycees inside the prison walls. Membership of the 'jailbird' Jaycees jumped from fifty to more than 650 men in just eighteen months. He worked in the kitchen and within months, was the prison's head cook. He also secured a hike in pay for convicts working in the prison's mess hall and worked on myriad projects to improve conditions for other inmates. Gacy's finest moment came in the summer of 1969 when he oversaw the construction of a miniature golf course for the prisoners in the recreation yard. He was generally seen as a 'model prisoner'.

'He had no particular problem during his stay,' warden Calvin Auger said in 1979. 'His adjustment was exceptionally good. He was a good worker, a willing worker with only one minor disciplinary thing on his record, just a hassle with another resident with nobody injured.' Auger added that routine psychological examinations of Gacy 'didn't show anything that was abnormal'. While he was in prison, there was no evidence of the predatory activity that had seen him jailed or that would later be forever attached to the name John Wayne Gacy.

Despite all his efforts, the first shot at parole in June 1969 was torpedoed by the parole board. That would not happen the next time. Gacy threw himself into his prison projects and had completed sixteen high-school courses and obtained his high-school diploma by November 1969. The next hearing was slated June 1970. He would be ready.

One of the most seismic events to occur during his incarceration was the death of his father, John Stanley Gacy, who went into a Chicago hospital days before Christmas in 1969. He died on Christmas Day at sixty-nine years of age. The cause of death was cirrhosis of the liver, no doubt a result of decades retreating to his basement lair and drinking himself into oblivion to try to forget the horrors he had seen on the Western Front in the First World War.

The spectre of John Stanley Gacy would haunt his son until his own death twenty-five years later but in 1967, his marriage, children and success had seemed to soften the old man towards him. But, Gacy must have known that this would inevitably change with his conviction. When guards gave Gacy the bad news about the man who had tormented him – and shaped his twisted life – he collapsed to the cement floor, sobbing.

The death of his father hit Gacy surprisingly hard. The warden refused to spring him for the funeral and that made his passing that much harder. It's doubtful whether Gacy ever resolved the profoundly dysfunctional relationship he had with his father – the man who was supposed to love and care for him, but for most of his life showed him only scorn.

'In these letters he talked about things that disappointed him,' said Hill. 'His father died while he was in prison and he couldn't go to the funeral. His wife filed for divorce, and he was bitter that all his friends had forgotten him, because he had done a lot for people.'

On 18 June 1970, Gacy's parole was approved and he walked out of the prison. He would eventually be back, in another institution and a different state.

His former father-in-law, Fred Myers, was appalled when Gacy was released after serving so little of his ten-year sentence. He later told a reporter through a crack in his door: 'I can't understand why they would have let him out of prison in Iowa.' Gacy had never fooled Myers with his bluster; indeed, his father-in-law had always suspected something much, much darker lay beneath The Colonel's slick veneer.

Donald L. Olson of the Iowa State Board of Parole would not release Gacy's psychiatric reports to the media years later, but said 'if there were any red flags, he wouldn't have been paroled.' The former Jaycees up-and-comer had obviously impressed the parole board. It would not be the first – or last – time Gacy would bamboozle the authorities and laymen alike.

'You can't judge a crook by its cover,' James Alan Fox, dean of the College of Criminal Justice at Boston's Northeastern University and an authority on multiple homicide offenders, told the *Waterloo Courier* in 1994. 'If serial killers were glassy-eyed lunatics then there would be no danger because people would avoid them. But the fact is they blend in very well. Many of them have jobs and families and they go to church on Sunday and kill part-time as a hobby. They usually kill their victims to cover up the dark side of their life. In Gacy's case, literally burying the evidence of their crimes.'

On the day he was released from prison, his old Jaycees friend Charley Hill picked him up from the Riverview Release Center in Newton, Iowa. Once again, Gacy insisted on his innocence to Hill and his wife over dinner at Nino's Family Restaurant. It was the same old Gacy.

Hill offered him a job in the hotel he ran but the very next day – barely a dozen hours later – Gacy walked into his friend's office and informed him he was leaving for Chicago to tend to his sick mother. 'I'll be back in Waterloo in a few days,' Gacy told his friend. But Gacy never came back. The two men, however, continued to stay in touch for a few years.

Gacy returned to Chicago and moved in with his mom, taking a job at Bruno's Restaurant and Lounge at 126 N. Wells in the city's famed Loop area. The joint was a favourite of players for the Chicago Blackhawks hockey team. Gacy would get his old buddy, Hill, tickets and he even introduced him to some of Hawks stars who sank beer at Bruno's. But, after Christmas 1972, Hill never heard from Gacy again.

7

The Seventies

The sixties had brought unrest and change to Chicago. There were protests against the Vietnam War, civil-rights marches and the blowout that was the 1968 Democratic Convention, when the streets exploded in rage. Economically, the shift from heavy industry and manufacturing was also causing havoc as the vast army of blue-collar workers, particularly on the South Side, watched as steel mills and factories closed their doors. In 1971, the famed Union Stock Yards, which at one point had employed tens of thousands of people, slaughtered their last head of cattle. And Chicago was no longer the hog butcher to the world.

Everywhere one looked, the city was changing and society was changing along with it. Chicago, always a tough town, was getting tougher by the day. By the late sixties, the murder rate was exploding, peaking in 1974 with 970 recorded cases. Many of the victims were African-American and the bloodshed was mainly in the South and West Sides of the city.

Under manager Leo Durocher, the beloved Chicago Cubs finished third in the National League East, while their South Side rivals, the White Sox, finished under .500. In the 1971–2 season, hockey's Chicago Blackhawks were ousted in four straight games by the New York Rangers. Basketball's Chicago Bulls lost four straight games in the play-offs to the Los Angeles Lakers. The beloved Bears of the NFL finished with a dismal 6–8 record.

This was the city to which John Wayne Gacy, now twenty-nine years old, returned after a jolt in an Iowa prison. He hoped to put his jail time and his crimes behind him. He moved back in with his mother, Marion, in the family's North Side home and began work at Bruno's Restaurant; the skills he had picked up managing the KFCs and as head cook in prison served him well. Among Gacy's multitude of sins, sloth was not one of them. He had been a hard worker as a kid, as a KFC manager and as head cook for hundreds of convicts. And he was a hustler. No matter what project he was embarking on, Gacy always gave 150%. While he manned the grill at Bruno's at night, he started looking for side gigs to supplement his income – and to fill his time.

But there was something else gnawing at John Wayne Gacy. Those old inner demons had never been vanquished, the sexual and violent urges were back – if they had ever left.

In 1971, most gay men and women remained firmly in the closet for fear of being rejected by their families or having their lives obliterated. But times were changing. The Stonewall Riots in New York City in the summer of 1969 had made gay people more visible, the crack in the closet door was widening. Chicago had always had gay and lesbian bars near the Loop on the Near North and Near South Sides of the city. Here, gay people could unwind and be themselves and, as a bonus, the pick-up scene was thriving. Lots of young servicemen, transients and hippies were on the move in those days. And John Wayne Gacy knew it.

Chicago's massive Greyhound Bus Terminal at the corner of Clark and Randolph in the Loop opened on 19 March 1953, having cost a whopping $10 million to build, a fortune for the time. The five-storey building took up the entire block and, as a bonus, there was a Toffenetti's restaurant next to the station. With outlets in Chicago and New York, the eatery was a favourite. It had a huge staff of 250 workers and could serve 600 patrons at a time. There were also eighteen shops selling various things in the glittering new edifice. For years, the station delivered, but changes were coming to the Loop and by the late 1960s the area had become more of a commercial area during the day, but at night the area filled up with junkies, sex workers, muggers, vagrants and teen runaways.

By the seventies, the Greyhound Terminal, like swathes of Chicago, was on the skids. The 25 November 1975 edition of the *Chicago Tribune* carried the headline 'The Bus For Rapists, Pickpockets, and Vagrants Is Now Loading' and it landed with a thud. The article read: 'A couple of years ago, when tsk-tsking about the Loop and how it "just isn't safe at night" was at its peak, one of the truly unsafe places downtown was the Greyhound bus station, at Clark and Randolph Streets. It attracted all sorts of undesirables: pimps in search of new girls, pickpockets and purse-snatchers after fast cash, "midnight cowboys" on the prowl for homosexuals, rapists hunting prey, baggage thieves watching for easy pickings, con artists in need of "pigeon drop" victims, bums looking for a place to drink and flop.' By that time there was a women and children's safety zone in the terminal, which was overseen by security staff.

For a predator like John Wayne Gacy, the area around the bus station became a target-rich environment. But even hardened Chicagoans avoided the place – viewing it as beyond the pale – until, finally, it was demolished in 1989.

It was in the area of the terminal on 12 February 1971 that John Wayne Gacy's old desires reasserted themselves. He was still working at Bruno's, which was in the area, and he was only eight months out of prison.

A young boy told cops that Gacy had picked him up and tried to force him into sex. The lad was not interested and the physically imposing cook was arrested for assault. This time Gacy wriggled out of trouble. He told detectives that, being the good guy he is, he had simply picked up the boy who was hitch-hiking. The younger man had then tried to proposition the older man. Well, that was too much for Gacy and he threw the boy out of his car.

When the time came to go to court, the boy did not show up to testify. The charges against Gacy were dropped and, most importantly, the parole board in Iowa never learned about the incident that could have sent him back to jail for eight years to finish his sentence. If that had happened, scores of boys and young men would no doubt still be alive. One of the most shocking features of the later investigation into Gacy was the staggering number of times he slipped through the hands of the police. He was clever but he was also lucky. Also, cops in those days didn't have access to the databases that have become a signature of modern policing. Finding out if a villain had a past record or was wanted by another police force was no simple matter.

Gacy had another close call that summer. On 22 June 1971, he was arrested and charged with aggravated sexual battery and reckless conduct. The kid in question told detectives that Gacy had flashed a sheriff's badge, lured him into his car and forced him to perform oral sex. But when the kid subsequently tried to blackmail Gacy, the charges were dropped. The affair had all the earmarks that Gacy would come to be known for.

That year his mother had loaned him the money to buy the bungalow at 8213 West Summerdale Avenue near the village of Norridge in Norwood Park Township, an unincorporated area of Cook County. Marion Gacy moved in with her beloved Johnny. Things were looking up for him. In addition to his job at Bruno's he had started doing maintenance and painting jobs on the side.

Despite the incidents with law enforcement, Gacy was looking for the opportunity to re-establish his veneer of respectability and he found it in a friend of his younger sister, Carole Hoff, whom he had dated in high school. She was a frequent visitor in the Gacy home. He wanted some kind of domestic cover for his less savoury nocturnal activities – 'Hey, I'm married!'– and perhaps he longed for more children.

Carole was a pretty blonde woman who had recently divorced. She had two young daughters and she was in a financial pinch and desperate to provide for her girls. When Hoff and Gacy reconnected in 1971, she started to think about her high-school paramour in a romantic way. Gacy had been like a brother and she liked visiting him and his mother. She later said she liked listening to him talk. He was hard-working, he was kind and most importantly, good to her children. 'He swept me off my feet,' she told the *New York Times* in 1978. When her divorce was finalised that year, he was there to pick up the pieces. It was Gacy's mother Marion who, when she heard Carole was having a tough time paying her rent, suggested that she and her two daughters move into their new home on West Summerdale Avenue.

Gacy was truthful with Hoff – to a point. He came clean about his troubles in Iowa, telling her it was a terrible mistake, a once-in-a-lifetime kind of thing. In the summer of 1971, the aspiring contractor proposed to the attractive divorcee and she accepted – even though they hadn't been dating long. In October 1971, Gacy's parole ended and in November, the records of his previous criminal convictions were sealed. Unknown to Carole, their engagement did not curtail Gacy's jaunts to the Loop looking for runaways and young hustlers. Not by a long shot. And what Hoff didn't know – couldn't have known – was that during their engagement, Gacy would murder for the first time.

For years, detectives called the teenage victim the 'Greyhound Bus Boy'. After he attended a family party on the night of 2 January 1972, Gacy decided to drive his big, black Oldsmobile down to the Civic Center in the Loop to check out the spectacular ice sculptures. Past midnight, the rough-hewn denizens of the area were out in full force. One of them was a sixteen-year-old boy en route to his home in Omaha, Nebraska, after a holiday visit with an aunt and uncle in Michigan. There was a lay-over at the Greyhound Station and the curious teen – who was well-travelled – decided to take a look around while he waited for his connecting bus. Then the hand of fate conspired to deliver the teenager into the arms of a fledgling predator. Gacy would later confess that he lured sixteen-year-old Timothy Jack McCoy from the terminal and into his Oldsmobile.

'Hey, kid, wanna see Chicago?'

It was cold and Gacy seemed kindly – it's not hard to see why the boy might have been persuaded. Gacy took the boy on a sightseeing tour of the metropolis. Gacy's mother Marion was spending the night at his sister's house, so Gacy had the place to himself and he drove the boy to his suburban home. Naive McCoy thought he would have a bite and spend the night at Gacy's then would be taken back to the Greyhound Terminal in the morning so he could catch the bus onwards to Omaha.

Gacy later said that, when they got back to the cozy ranch house in the suburbs, he made the boy a few drinks with grain alcohol. What load of nonsense the older man then told his new young friend is not known but Gacy said he and McCoy had consensual oral sex and then retired to separate bedrooms.

The future serial killer insisted that he had no intention of murdering McCoy but that would change the next day. Gacy told detectives he awoke the next morning and there was McCoy standing in the doorway of his bedroom. The boy had a kitchen knife in his hand.

The former convict – not long out of prison – said he jumped from his bed and the young man raised his hands in surrender. But the knife – tilted upwards – caught Gacy on the forearm. The older man then twisted the knife from his guest's hand and slammed his head into the wall before kicking him against the wardrobe. Gacy approached the boy and McCoy, now terrified, kicked Gacy in the stomach, doubling him over.

'Motherfucker! I'll kill you!' Gacy screamed at the boy before wrestling him to the ground and repeatedly stabbing him in the chest as he straddled him.

As McCoy was dying in the bedroom, his killer took the knife to the bathroom where he washed off the teen's blood. Gacy then entered his kitchen and noticed on the counter a carton of eggs, some bacon and the table set for two. The boy had been making the man who would end his life some breakfast.

The former Jaycee said several years after he was arrested that, after killing the teen, he felt 'totally drained'. But … and this is a big but, as he listened to the 'gurgulations' of a dying McCoy, Gacy had experienced a 'mind-numbing orgasm'.

'That's when I realised that death was the ultimate thrill,' Gacy said.

In what would become his modus operandi, Gacy dumped McCoy's lifeless body into the crawl space under his house through a trap door. Days later, he would bury him in the dirt coffin below.

This would be the only time Gacy stabbed to death one of his victims, the rest were strangled. William Kunkle, the chief prosecutor at Gacy's trial years later, said that the murder of McCoy was the killer's only deviation in killing over thirty-three victims.

Even as he relished the murder of McCoy, Gacy had a plan for himself. A few months before her son's wedding, Gacy's mother rented an apartment and moved out of the house leaving the lovebirds alone. On 1 July 1972, Gacy married Carole Hoff and she and the girls moved into what would become the house of death at 8213 West Summerdale Avenue. Now, he could have it both ways.

Carole never found out that, just nine days before their wedding, Gacy had been arrested again. The details had a familiar ring: a teen boy told cops that Gacy informed him he was a Cook County Deputy Sheriff, flashed his badge and ordered him into his Oldsmobile. There the boy was forced to perform oral sex on the bogus cop. When the kid jumped out of the car and tried to make a run for it, Gacy tried to run him down. Bizarrely, the charges were again dropped.

Gacy and Carole Hoff settled into married life. She was impressed by how good he was with the girls. There was one problem, though. It didn't take long for Carole to notice the stench coming from the crawl space underneath the bungalow. Swarms of flies infested the back room of their home. Carole thought that maybe the flies were attracted to something rotting below the floors.

Gacy, of course, had an explanation. He told his new bride that the foul smell was actually run-off from a broken sewer pipe and he would take care of it. Gacy spread lime in the dark crypt to try and temper the smell but the stomach-churning stench only got worse. McCoy was the first victim to be buried in the crawl space and Chief Prosecutor Kunkle noted that 'when his second wife moved into the house and complained of odours in the basement, he took the opportunity when she was out of town to cover that first body with concrete.' Pouring concrete over young Timothy Jack McCoy's resting place meant that the flies hit the road. The smell remained but it was not as bad as before.

Carole later recalled that, over the span of their short marriage, Gacy would sometimes go into the crawl space armed with bags of lime. Yet the blustering Gacy would always scoff at the very idea there was a smell emanating from the area. 'There was no smell,' he later insisted, other than a musty odour at times. 'People were in and out of that house daily for years. And other than when it rained, there was no odour and certainly not like what some of the books said. That's all fantasy. If that odour was there somebody would have noticed it sooner.'

Things were going well for Gacy, all things considered. He was rebuilding his life, and it looked like his new contracting business had legs. He called it P. D. M. – for Painting Decorating Maintenance. By the middle of 1973, the company was doing enough business for Gacy to concentrate on it full time and give up his job behind the grill at Bruno's in the Loop. As his small business prospered, Gacy eventually took over the garage of the home for equipment and supplies. It was off-limits to his wife and his two stepdaughters.

Carole and John had also become close friends with their new neighbours, the Grexas. Whenever Gacy threw a party, they were always there. However, they also noticed the stench coming from the otherwise tidy home. For her part, Lillie Grexa suspected that a rat had died beneath the floor. She told Gacy that he should take care of it.

The Grexas also noted something else about the Gacys. At P. D. M. Contractors, Gacy tended to hire teenage boys – he said it was because they were cheap. The other, more sinister, reason was not yet apparent. Sometimes the boys would be in and out of the home at all hours.

'Well, we knew something was going on. When you see young kids hanging around the house at all hours, until all hours, you've got to think something,' Ed Grexa later said. 'His wife, Carole, so much as told me. I was over helping to fix their washer. I was just joking around, you know, and I said, "You've been married quite a while now. When are there going to be some kids?" She said, "Well, to do that, you've got to sleep together. John doesn't. John likes his boys."'

The Grexas had six children and one of Grexa's boys worked for Gacy and was even propositioned by him. That was all before December 1978. Nevertheless, they couldn't quite wrap their heads around what was eventually revealed about their friend and neighbour.

'He was a nice guy. He was a good, warm neighbour. Helping all the time,' Ed Grexa said after Gacy was arrested for murder. 'Having parties for as many as 400 people on his driveway and his front lawn. He certainly didn't act as if there was anything wrong with him.'

His wife later added: 'I feel this is all a bad dream and I'm going to wake up. When I do, the John Gacy I used to know will be inviting Ed and me over to have a drink in his house.'

The Gacys would throw massive theme parties. Gacy threw a luau-themed party and there was a Western bash. They were well attended and fun. Gacy's parties were always a success. And Gacy was revelling in his transformation from ex-con to, once again, being a respected businessman and a well-liked neighbour.

Gacy was increasingly involved with the community and had become a member of the Moose Lodge, another service club known for good deeds and boozing. He was always willing to lend a hand or his tools to anyone who needed them. During the cold and snowy Chicago winters, he would plough his neighbours' sidewalks and driveways free of charge. And he was more involved than ever in the Democratic Party in suburban Chicago.

On the surface, everything seemed perfect at 8213 W. Summerdale Ave., aside from the stench, of course. But Carole noticed that her husband was spending less and less time at home. He was out most nights. Where was he and what did he do during these evening sojourns? Gacy told Carole that it was work. He was dealing with suppliers, checking out construction sites and jobs he planned to bid on, or he was talking to potential customers.

After the first year of their marriage, the couple's sex life petered off to non-existent, which seemed odd for a man in the prime of his life. And there was something else. Beneath the kitchen sink, Carole found a stack of magazines featuring naked men. One of the featured photos was of a young man who appeared to be covered in blood. On another occasion, Carole later recalled, she found a number of wallets belonging to teenage boys in the Oldsmobile. When she confronted her husband about these things he reacted with anger. These accusations, these slurs were all too much for John Wayne Gacy.

'He would throw furniture,' she later recalled. 'He broke a lot of my furniture. I think now, if there were murders, some must have taken place when I was in that house.'

But there were still those old urges gnawing away at him. By 1975 he had told his wife he was bisexual. After Gacy and Carole had carnal relations on Mother's Day that May, he told her that it would be 'the last time' they would ever have sex. It was one promise he kept. The couple were entering the twilight of their marriage and it would be all over by early 1976. They would eventually divorce on 2 March, after just under four years of what had not been wedded bliss. Carole would cite John's infidelity with other women as the reason for the divorce.

Carole couldn't have known, as her marriage started to disintegrate in 1975, that Gacy had been fantasising over the death of McCoy for years. It was a thrill he was desperate to relive. And he would relive it. In 1975, he had already murdered his second victim.

8

Ch-Ch-Changes

John Wayne Gacy lived a double life that was shocking in its jarring contradictions. On the one hand, there was John Wayne Gacy, the glad-handing, affable businessman and neighbour whose energy and hustle seemed boundless. He was always ready to lend a hand with a smile. Involved in his community, he was charitable, generous and likeable. And then there was the Gacy that only a few saw: the cruel, sexually driven monster who used the former to disguise the latter's vile deeds.

In many ways, Gacy was the quintessential serial killer. In others, he was not. Hollywood typically portrays serial killers as the creepy neighbour not necessarily playing with a full deck, or a transient killer roaming from state to state to seek out new hunting grounds. Gacy was neither of those things. But nor was Ted Bundy. Nor was Gary Ridgway, the Green River Killer.

'The majority of serial killers are not reclusive, social misfits who live alone. They are not monsters and may not appear strange,' an FBI symposium on serial killers reported. 'Many serial killers hide in plain sight within their communities. Serial murderers often have families and homes, are gainfully employed, and appear to be normal members of the community.

Because many serial murderers can blend in so effortlessly, they are oftentimes overlooked by law enforcement and the public.'

Gacy carefully constructed an outward appearance and demeanour as a jolly, blue-collar guy who loved his family and community, and there's something to that too in the observations by the FBI: 'The interpersonal traits include glibness, superficial charm, a grandiose sense of self-worth, pathological lying, and the manipulation of others. The affective traits include a lack of remorse and/or guilt, shallow affect, a lack of empathy and failure to accept responsibility. The lifestyle behaviours include stimulation-seeking behaviour, impulsivity, irresponsibility, parasitic orientation, and a lack of realistic life goals.' Again, these are all traits we can clearly see in Gacy.

The report goes on to say more: 'The anti-social behaviours include poor behavioural controls, early childhood behaviour problems, juvenile delinquency, revocation of conditional release, and criminal versatility. The combination of these individual personality traits, interpersonal styles, and socially deviant lifestyles are the framework of psychopathy and can manifest themselves differently in individual psychopaths.'

John Wayne Gacy maintained until the bitter end that he was too busy to kill. Indeed, in addition to the rape and murder of more than thirty-three young men, he was able to turn P. D. M. Contracting into a $250,000-per-year business; be an active member of his local Moose Lodge and a player in the Democratic Party; and an engaged and social member of his community. Whilst Gacy presented his life as a moderate success story it was – all of it – painfully average and normal.

And Gacy is not alone among serial killers for his outward hyper-normalcy. Dennis Rader fits neatly into this category. Rader was a Boy Scout leader and the president of his church congregation. He was also a loving husband and a dedicated, warm father. He served a non-eventful stint in the United States

Air Force and found work as an electrician when he returned to Wichita, Kansas. Rader even met his wife Paula at church. But, like John Wayne Gacy, Rader lived a double life. Rader was also the notorious BTK (bind torture kill) killer responsible for the torture and murder of ten people including children between 1974 and 1991. When he was finally arrested in 2005, his wife, children and friends refused to believe the shocking news.

'My dad was the one who taught me my morals,' his stunned daughter Kerri would later say. 'He taught me right from wrong.'

But outward appearances can be deceiving, something Rader himself would admit in 2005. Beneath his everyman veneer lurked a sexual sadist. 'Sexual, sexual fantasies. Probably more than normal. All males probably go through some kind of, uh, sexual fantasy. Mine was just probably a bit weirder than other people,' Rader later confessed, admitting that he would bind his own hands and ankles for practice.

Rader's killing spree overlapped with Gacy's. He murdered his first victim about two years after John Wayne Gacy murdered Timothy McCoy. On 15 January 1974, as his own family slept, Rader slipped out of the door of his modest home. The victims would be the Otero family. The husband and wife were murdered as their children watched in horror. Josie, eleven, was then dragged to the basement, had her underwear pulled off and was hung from a sewer pipe. When the terrified child asked Rader what was going to happen to her. He coldly replied: 'Well, honey, you're going to be in heaven tonight with the rest of your family.' As the little girl choked to death, Rader masturbated, then took photos of the dead and the child's underwear as a trophy of his first kill.

And just like that, Rader returned home and got ready for church.

More murders would follow that first taste of the ultimate thrill. Kathryn Bright in April 1974, Shirkey Van and Nancy

Fox in 1977. Marine Hedge in 1985 and Vicki Wegerie in 1986 and finally Dolores Davis in 1991. Rader and his wife had two children and Rader put murder on the shelf while he became the best dad he could and this explained the gaps between some of the murders.

'I was so excited, for us and our folks. We were now a family. With a job and a baby, I got busy,' he later told detectives. For several years, the death machine remained idle as Rader fronted a happy, well-adjusted family. People around Wichita knew about BTK but no one thought it could be Dennis Rader.

After he was arrested in 2005, his wife Paula told cops that Rader was 'a good man, a great father. He would never hurt anyone.'

Rader went on to confess to the ten murders. If Kansas had had the death penalty, he would surely have been executed by lethal injection. Instead, he was sentenced to 175 years in prison without the possibility of parole. But this pleasantly plain man was a monster. The struggle to deal with the truth of what Rader was must have surely been the hardest for his family. 'Should I tell you that I grew up adoring you, that you were the sunshine of my life?' Kerri wrote in her autobiography, *A Serial Killer's Daughter*. 'I just wished you were sitting next to me in the theatre, sharing a tub of buttered popcorn. But you're not.' And like the Rader clan, Gacy's own family were also stunned when it became clear the horrors he had inflicted on all those boys and young men.

Unless someone was looking for the serial killer in John Wayne Gacy – and looking very deep indeed – they were not going to find him. Serial killers like Rader and Gacy wear a 'mask of sanity' that hides the murderous mania within. When Ted Bundy was on trial for his life in Florida, even the judge was charmed. At sentencing he even expressed regret that Bundy had chosen murder instead of a career in law.

By the time he was executed in Florida's electric chair in 1989, Bundy had admitted to thirty victims. Many of them had been fooled into trusting him thanks to his good looks and charm. The truth is that most serial killers don't fit the Hollywood playbook. Most are painfully ordinary, but extraordinarily successful at hiding their chilling secrets. 'They [serial killers] tend to blend into society relatively efficiently … that's another thing people are disturbed by,' said Dr. Jeffrey Walsh, a criminal justice professor at Illinois State University. 'Because of how horrible their acts often are, we sometimes think they look different than us or that we would recognise them. The fact is, many of them have regular lives and blend in, so they don't meet the stereotypical views of what a monster would be like.'

According to the Serial Killer Information Center, only about 12.5% of known serial killers fit the profile of the classic, twenty-something, white, male trope beloved by screenwriters. And that's from a study of nearly 4,700 mass murderers carried out at Radford University. Many serial killers are married, educated and employed. It is this normalcy that acts as their accomplice over the years, and even decades, that they go undetected.

One of those killers hiding in plain sight was Joseph James DeAngelo Jr. – who for forty years evaded capture before finally being revealed as the Golden State Killer – previously known as the Original Night Stalker, the East Area Rapist and the Visalia Ransacker. He was married to a lawyer and together they raised three daughters. He had even worked as a cop. But after dark, the evil that possessed the Citrus Heights, California man would emerge, ready to wreak havoc.

When cops finally nabbed him, DeAngelo was cooking a roast for his daughter and granddaughter. He pleaded guilty to thirteen murders on 29 June 2020, after prosecutors took the death penalty off the table. His arrest was the result of decades of efforts by law enforcement, independent investigators, survivors and victims' families. They never stopped looking for the murderer and found him living in the very area that had been his hunting ground. He was identified through DNA.

Detective Sergeant Jason Moran of the Cook County Sheriff's Department is now the keeper of the flame for the remaining unidentified victims of Gacy recovered from West Summerdale Avenue. Using DNA technology, the search goes on to try and give their families answers. He maintains that Gacy's ordinariness is what made the killer so terrifying. '[The public] would feel much more comfortable if Gacy was this type of creepy, sequestered ghoul that was unkempt and heinous,' Moran said in 2020. 'But instead, he dressed as a clown and bounced kids on his knee. He would knock at your door and say vote for my candidate.'

Gacy was always ready with an excuse or lie for any awkward questions. Odd comings and goings and late-night visits from young men, workers digging trenches underneath the house – he was always lightning-quick with an explanation. Lying was second nature to him.

He had a knack for building trust with people and he used this with those young men and boys who would later become his victims and be buried in the mass grave under his house. 'He often would build up trust with his victims, so they wouldn't need to be on guard,' Jason Moran said. 'He was their employer, their friend. He may have been someone who provided them with alcohol and drugs and maybe a place to sleep at night. That's an easy way to kill someone.'

Moran's mentor and retired Sheriff's investigator, Phil Betticker recalled the massive theme parties at Gacy's home. He bitterly noted that the attendees were celebrating on top of Gacy's own private graveyard. 'He'd have parties at his residence where he'd invite maybe 200 people. He'd be the centre of attraction,' Betticker said. 'One on one, or in a group setting, he would be the last person that you'd think was a serial killer and as devious as he was.'

Former Cook County Judge Sam Amirante was a friend of Gacy and defended him in his murder trial in 1980. The Killer Clown was his first client in private practice. Gacy's everyman charm, Amirante said, was the key to his success as a serial predator. 'I always tell people that the scary thing about Gacy was that he wasn't scary at all. That's the scary thing – he could have been anyone's brother or father, uncle,' Amirante said. 'He was not an intimidating kind of person, with the exception of when he would turn and change out of the very affable, charming, likeable guy into the killer that he was.'

In his 2011 book, *John Wayne Gacy: Defending a Monster*, Amirante wrote, 'Everyone who ever knew John Gacy knew one thing about him – he was a master manipulator. He could sell ice cubes to Eskimos.'

Amirante probably got to know Gacy as well as anyone. His client's fabled pedestrian side could quickly slide away and in its place, a new frightening face and tone. Once, when Gacy was drunk, he confessed to Amirante that he was 'judge, jury and executioner of many, many people'. 'He looked at his victims like he was taking out the trash. He had no feelings about them,' Amirante said, more than forty years after his client had unburdened himself in that late night confession. But Amirante later admitted that it took months for him to unravel Gacy's true, sinister nature. 'He could talk about a child who's dying of cancer and cry like a baby about this child he didn't even know or never met and feel authentically sad about this child. Then he'd talk about another child that he murdered and have no feelings whatsoever,' he said.

Psychiatrist Dr. Richard Rappaport spent countless hours with Gacy. His job was to save the killer's life while he was on trial in 1980. Failure would mean the electric chair or a lethal injection for Gacy. He tried to explain the disconnect between the perception of the loveable Mr. Gacy and the reviled serial killer. Rappaport told the court that Gacy had a 'borderline personality and a slew of psychosexual disorders, including fetishism, sexual sadism and necrophilia'. In addition to this, Gacy had both narcissistic and antisocial disorders.

According to Rappaport, Gacy would have brief psychotic meltdowns triggered by a deep rage within him. The targets of his rage? Young men and boys. 'He thought these boys were him and he was the father,' Rappaport said, adding that ultimately, Gacy's screaming rage was actually aimed at himself. It was the stern ghost of his father, John Stanley Gacy, rearing his head from the grave. Rappaport went so far as to theorise that the reason Gacy stashed his victims in the crawl space was because John Stanley would put his son's toys in the basement as punishment. The dead were 'love objects'.

Yet, Rappaport stopped short of stating that the ordinary-looking man in the dock was necessarily 'insane'. Gacy was 'sufficiently in touch with reality so that he realised he had to provide for his habits, he had to provide a receptacle for getting rid of these [shells] of people,' Rappaport said.

As for why Gacy killed so many times, the doctor said he didn't believe there was a 'psychoanalytic' answer. He added that the killer's stated motivations: fear of being unmasked as a killer, blackmail or being outed as a homosexual didn't jibe with his own theories. '[Gacy may have] imposed those ideas on the individuals [or] tried to elicit behaviour on their part to conform to his idea that they were bad people. That was part of the projective identification that I was explaining before,' the forensic psychiatrist testified.

Furthermore, Gacy did not suffer from multiple-personality syndrome. The inner rage and demons that had tormented

Gacy were 'intense expressions of hostility, the defendant could justify his behaviour as conforming to his private code of morality, even though he recognised that his behaviour would not be considered socially acceptable'. Rappaport added that Gacy's antisocial personality allowed him to simply forget his criminal actions and the horrors he committed with his own hands. And then he'd transform back into John Wayne Gacy, the good neighbour, generous friend, and community-spirited individual that was his Dr Jekyll. He would return to the Moose Lodge, the Poland Parade Committee and his work with the Chicago Democratic machine without blinking.

A collection of tapes recorded by Sam Amirante and his co-counsel, Robert Motta, as they spoke with Gacy are an instructive journey inside the mind of a homicidal maniac. They were recorded several months after Gacy was arrested in 1978 and he became one of the most infamous people in the world. These conversations with evil took place in the Cook County Jail's Cermak Hospital, where Gacy was housed following his arrest. Motta gave the tapes to his son Bob, also a lawyer, when he turned twenty-one and he would eventually turn them into a podcast series that explores the darkness that was John Wayne Gacy.

Notable from the conversations, is the fact that the client appears to believe he's smarter than his own lawyers and is clearly trying to manipulate them. The killer next door had admitted everything to Amirante shortly after Des Plaines cops arrested him but during these talks we hear Gacy starting to walk back the earlier confession. He insists he doesn't remember the murders and begins blaming others. He even claims another individual was involved in the murders: Jack Hanley. It becomes clear that he is developing an alter ego.

The tapes reveal a man with little remorse. 'He was absolutely a sociopath,' Bob Motta told NBC in 2021. 'And his inability to have any kind of empathy was chilling.'

At one point in the tapes, the elder Motta asks his client, 'Did you ever have the feeling that God wouldn't care if these people were dead because they were prostitutes or having sex for money?'

Gacy responds: 'No, but you want to know something? I can recall that more than once I wanted to pray. Not pray for me, but pray for them, for being such a lost soul, for being so stupid.' In the end, Gacy believed his victims had no one to blame but themselves for their final hours of torment. He told his shocked lawyers: 'Yes, there's not one of them that didn't die ... that I'm aware of ... that didn't die through their own hand or their own wrongdoing. If you want to say I tempted them, put them into temptation – yes. Because, understand this, everybody that ever came to my house, there was never a struggle and nobody was ever forced into my house ... Everybody came to my house willingly, understandably and knowing what's going to happen.'

At other times, he speculates what might have or could have happened at his suburban home. 'He would say, "I went to bed. I was hammered. I woke up. And there's a dead body in my house,"' Motta said, quoting Gacy. '"So I assume I killed them, I just don't remember killing them." Gacy was always the smartest guy in the room. Or so he thought.'

By early 1976, with Carole Hoff and her kids gone, John Wayne Gacy was unleashed . He would continue to balance the two extremes in his troubled life. And he was about to get even better at both of them. His younger sister, Karen, later said she noticed a change in her brother around the time he and Carole divorced. 'Something in their marriage just started to break,' Karen said. 'He always had a way of pushing people away, and I think that that's what he did. Maybe it was a protection mode for her and the children.' But nothing could prepare her for what her brother was going to do.

Karen will go to her grave remembering every minute detail of that day in December 1978. 'I just sat there and didn't know what to do. I had to talk to my mother,' she recalled. 'We cried and we hugged, and neither of us could believe it because it wasn't the person we knew. He was always good and kind and always taking care of us.'

John Wayne Gacy had spilled his guts to detectives and his legal team when he was first arrested. And then he recanted. He was innocent, he claimed. And that was his tune until the minute an executioner jabbed a needle into his arm. While he awaited the inevitable on death row in Illinois, Karen recalls that her brother confessed that he wasn't guilty of *all* of the murders – maybe just one or two. 'Well, then you're guilty of all because you can't kill one and not be guilty,' she had responded. Later she admitted, 'I felt kind of cheated in a way because I didn't know part of him.'

And of the killer's many appeals that failed to save his life? 'I had always said to my husband and my family that if any appeal ever worked, I'd see to it that he never walked the face of the earth again,' she said. '… because I did love him as a brother, but I didn't like anything about what he did.'

Karen admitted she felt guilt for decades even though she had no hand in nor any knowledge of the heinous crimes committed by her brother. 'I don't want other people that have a son or a daughter that do something, I don't want them to think that they're a bad parent. People have choices after they're a certain age, and if they make the right choices, their life is good.'

John Wayne Gacy had choices. He chose to murder.

9

The Many Mr Gacys

In the year 1974 in the United States, the long war in Vietnam that had claimed more than 58,000 American lives was now in the past and the civil unrest of the 1960s had ebbed. But the country was in upheaval. That January, increasingly embattled U. S. President Richard Nixon cited executive privilege in his refusal to surrender more than 500 audiotapes and documents relating to a break-in at the Democratic Party headquarters at the Watergate Hotel complex in Washington, DC. On a daily basis, Americans were bombarded with new revelations about the criminal machinations emanating from the White House, even as Nixon assured them their president was 'not a crook'. By the end of January, in his State of the Union address, Nixon was urging Americans to put Watergate behind them, saying 'one year of Watergate is enough.' But by August, it was all over and he resigned in disgrace.

The energy crisis that crippled the free movement of Americans was just around the corner that summer. *Happy Days*, a long-running comedy about the 1950s, made its debut on ABC.

And in suburban Chicago, John Wayne Gacy committed his second murder.

Still his wife at this time, Carole had become accustomed to the nocturnal movements of her go-getter husband. Little did she know that he was cruising for sex with young men and boys. Carole and her two daughters must have been away from the house at some point in January because, once again, Gacy's suburban bungalow became a crime scene – a house of death and despair.

The victim has, to this day, not been identified. After his arrest Gacy later confessed to detectives and so his account is all we know. Gacy recalled that the boy – estimated to have been between fourteen and eighteen years old – had brown, curly hair. After torturing and raping his victim, Gacy strangled him to death – this became his chosen method to dispatch his victims. When the boy was dead, Gacy stuffed his body in one of his home's storage closets. He told detectives that fluids leaked from the boy's mouth and nose and they stained the carpet. In future, the neophyte serial killer decided he would stuff his victim's socks or underwear into their mouths to stop the leakage. At other times, he would use a rag. Eventually, Gacy buried his second victim near his backyard barbecue pit, where he entertained politicians, local businessmen, friends and neighbours.

At this point, January 1974, Gacy still had constraints on his sinister sexual desires and bloodlust. Firstly, Carole and her daughters were still living with him. He was also very busy. His gambit to start P. D. M. Contractors had paid off in spades and he was now a full-time contractor. He wasn't lying about how hard he was hustling – often working fourteen- to sixteen-hour days. Even his probation officer had signed off on Gacy's new venture which made it necessary for him to work nights. At first, the gregarious Gacy got work from friends and family: minor repair work, some signage, laying concrete and even decorating. Later, the operation did interior design, landscaping and a host of other household assignments. Not only was Gacy putting in long hours, the work turned out to be very lucrative and opened up more opportunities for him. If Gacy had been a night owl before, he was even more nocturnal now. He was never home until the early morning hours.

It was also during these days that Gacy began developing the persona that would chill millions to the bone. The Chicago contractor's legacy would play a starring role in the tears of many professional and amateur clowns when he decided to get into clowning himself. Gacy heard through his Moose Lodge that there was something called the Jolly Joker Clown Club. The group regularly performed at fundraisers, local parties, parades and most importantly, the group would entertain sick children at Chicago-area hospitals. For some reason it appealed to the contractor. Gacy signed on in late 1975 and clowning would become his sinister signature.

He created two separate clown personas. One was Pogo the Clown, described as a happy-go-lucky jester while his other creation, Patches, was more serious, sad and frightening. Gacy later admitted that portraying his two clown characters allowed him to 'regress into childhood'. Sometimes, Gacy wouldn't even bother changing out of his clown outfits and would sit in Chicago watering holes in full make-up and costume.

'I took up the name Pogo,' Gacy said in the account he gave *The New Yorker*, 'and the reason was based on, one, that I was Polish, so that's where the "Po" [came from] – for Poles, and since I was on the go all the time, I took "go" and added it to it.'

It wasn't for the cash. The clowning was strictly a volunteer gig. He later told the FBI: 'The clowning was relaxation for me. I enjoyed entertaining kids … they [people] unwind in different ways, going out drinking or things like that. I could put on clown make-up and I was relaxed.'

When the truth was revealed about Gacy, it forever altered the way society looked at clowns. No longer did people see sad-sack, old circus jesters like Emmett Kelly Jr., TV's Bozo and Clarabelle or fast-food shill, Ronald McDonald. Instead, clowns became objects of terror. On the heels of Gacy came horror creations like Stephen King's malevolent clown, Pennywise, in his blockbuster novel *It*. The names 'Gacy', 'serial killer' and 'clown' are linked for eternity. A serial-killing clown? Thank John Wayne Gacy for that.

Psychology professor Dr. Martin Antony at Ryerson University in Toronto noted the change in culture around clowns when writing in the *Smithsonian Magazine* in 2013. 'You don't really see clowns in those kinds of safe, fun contexts anymore. You see them in movies and they're scary,' Antony told the publication. 'Kids are not exposed in that kind of safe, fun context as much as they used to be and the images in the media, the negative images, are still there.'

'We're comfortable with clowns in a specific context,' Benjamin Radford, author of *Bad Clowns*, told the Oxygen Network. 'If we see them at a party we say, "Oh, that's great," but if you see a clown at night in a vacant parking lot or knocking on your door at midnight, it's a different feeling.'

Radford also noted that the manner in which Gacy applied his make-up seems almost intentionally frightening. Author Mark Dery recognised the same in his book *The Pyrotechnic Insanitarium: American Culture on the Brink*. When Gacy was in costume 'complete with tasselled hat and creepy make-up − fiendish arched eyebrows and a smile that ends in evil, upswept points [professional clowns round off the corners of their smiles to avoid frightening children],' he didn't look like a friendly clown.

While there is no evidence Gacy ever murdered while in costume, his 'magic rope trick' and tricks with handcuffs doomed scores of young men to death. Putting his victims at ease by telling them he was going to show them one of his tricks, the Killer Clown would switch toy handcuffs for real ones. 'Once the victim was shackled and helpless, Gacy would subject him to horrific sexual abuse, torture, and ultimately death by ligature strangulation,' Dery wrote.

Even while he languished on death row, Gacy's fascination – or fetish – for clowns continued unabated. He sold paintings of clowns he claimed were his own to ghoulish crime fans.

Back in 1975, Gacy had a lot of balls in the air. His business, cruising for sex, a disintegrating marriage, his clowning, his work with the Moose Lodge and the bodies of two young men buried on his property. As his marriage staggered to its inevitable end, Gacy began cruising for action on a regular basis. He didn't bother to hide his activities.

One of his preferred hunting grounds was an area of Chicago called Uptown, a neighbourhood that had for decades been the first stop in the Windy City for poor southern whites looking for a leg-up on the socio-economic ladder. In a city known for its jazz and blues, country music could be heard in the air blasting out of Uptown dive bars. Like a lot of other inner-city neighbourhoods across America during the tumultuous upheaval of the fifties and sixties, the middle class had decided they had had enough of Uptown and fled to the city's suburbs. That left the poor, the luckless and people living on the fringe of mainstream America. Commuter rail and elevated train lines criss-crossed the area, as huge swathes of Uptown were torn down in the name of urban revitalisation. The housing – ageing, dowager mansions and low-rent hotels which had once housed the wives of sailors posted to the Great Lakes Naval Station during the Second World War – became hovels for the indigent. Residents now called the area 'Hillbilly Heaven'.

This was where John Wayne Gacy cruised the streets looking for sex with young men. Looking for victims. Another opportunity to do this unhindered by the presence of his family came when Carole went to help his mother, who had moved to Arkansas to be with Gacy's sister. In early 1975, his mother had broken her hip and dutiful daughter-in-law Carole offered to travel to Arkansas to lend a hand. Like a teenage boy, Gacy was delighted to have the place to himself.

Victim No. 3 was Gacy's eighteen-year-old P. D. M. employee John 'Johnny' Butkovich. After dropping out of school, Johnny had worked for Gacy for some months but wanted to quit. 'He did interior decorating for Gacy and slept over there several nights. We met him and he seemed like a nice guy,' Butkovich's mother said. 'After eight months he said he didn't want to work there any more. That's all he told us.' The young man, the child of Yugoslavian immigrants, was not happy with his boss in July 1975. Cops learned that the day before Butkovich disappeared, he had had an argument with Gacy about two weeks' back pay he was owed.

On 31 July 1975, Johnny Butkovich's parents reported that their son had disappeared. His car was found parked not far from Gacy's house. Butkovich's jacket and wallet were inside the car and the keys still in the ignition.

The missing boy's father called Gacy and the contractor volunteered to help find him, but he suggested Johnny had 'run away'. Again, Gacy was visited by detectives, and he had a story ready for them. According to the respected businessman, Johnny Butkovich and two pals had arrived at the contractor's home demanding the back pay. Gacy told cops they had reached a compromise and the trio had left in Butkovich's car.

Gacy would later admit the truth – that he saw the boy exiting his car, waving to get his attention. He approached his boss's car and told him point blank: 'I wanna talk to you.' By this time, Gacy was getting good at this game. He asked Butkovich to climb into his car and invited him back to the house where they would settle the contentious matter of the money owed.

Carole and his stepdaughters were away so he had the place to himself to do his absolute worst. He offered the kid a drink before showing the kid the old handcuff trick. Butkovich was now restrained and Gacy said he 'sat on the kid's chest for a while' before strangling him to death.

He stashed the body in his garage and the plan was that he would bury the corpse in the crawl space. But now, he had a problem. Carole and the girls decided they were going to return home earlier than they had initially planned. So Gacy was forced to improvise, something he had grown adept at. Butkovich was buried beneath the concrete floor of the extension in Gacy's garage that he would use as a tool room.

When their son went missing, the proud and tough Butkovich family were not going to give up. From the time their boy disappeared until his killer's arrest, the family phoned police more than a hundred times, desperately trying to convince them to take a closer look at Gacy. But the cops continually blew them off.

In the days following Gacy's arrest in December 1978, the Butkovich family was understandably bitter. 'If the police had only paid attention to us, they might have saved many lives,' his father Marco Butkovich told the *Chicago Tribune*. 'I'd like to know what good are all their damn computers if they can't put two and two together. We told the police to go there and investigate. But they didn't do it. I talked to Gacy on the phone after that [Johnny went missing] and he said the police never talked to him.' Cops also skipped talking to Butkovich's friends, Robert Otera and Joseph Meronicki, who witnessed the argument with Gacy the day before their friend went missing. And again, no one bothered to call officials in Iowa about Gacy.

As Gacy's killings escalated he was never far from police radar. Teens in the area would later tell cops about a man named 'John' cruising the area around Uptown looking for young hustlers. In January 1976, cops even staked out Gacy's home after a second young man in his employ went missing. They watched dozens of young men come and go from his modest Norwood Park home. Detectives asked the men and boys questions but they kept quiet. A 1976 report from the Rand Corporation think tank painted a disturbing picture of U. S. police indifference resulting in serial predators who were allowed to continue killing. 'Substantially more than half of all serious reported crimes receive no more than superficial attention from investigators,' concluded the three-volume study. And then it sat on a shelf gathering dust.

Did Chicago cops fail to join the dots on Gacy in these early years? University of Western Ontario criminology professor and author Michael Arntfield is an expert on cold cases and serial killers. He notes that the police took two different approaches to Gacy. Initially they were engaged in covert surveillance where they were hoping to collect evidence, but, he notes, 'when they [Des Plaines Police] finally get onto him they're pretty relentless, it's a good case of overt surveillance – just to make the person emotionally disintegrate. They made their movements known to deter him from doing anything else and he just went mad.'

Arntfield is one of the founders of the Murder Accountability Project, an organisation that charts homicidal patterns. What they watch for is 'murder clusters'. That's where a number of unsolved homicides have occurred that share geography, modus operandi and other homicidal aspects. He has collected information on a suspected serial killer preying on women on the South Side of Chicago from 1999 to 2018. The killer has become known as the Chicago Strangler. 'There have been fifty-one or fifty-two strangulations where the victims have either been posed or set on fire in a dumpster,' he said. 'Local police had no idea these might be connected. There's a very specific M.O.: a stranger set on fire, usually near transit hubs. That's just insane. None of them make the news and they're all scattered across different precincts … And they [police] are still officially saying, "We don't think it's a serial killer, they're all random murders."'

Just like reports to Chicago-area cops that they may have had a serial predator in their midst in the mid- to late-seventies, the violence and terror tactics of the People's Temple under the Reverend Jim Jones were ignored. No action was taken regarding Jones until the mass 'suicide' in the jungle in 1978.

While cops would later acknowledge they missed the signals they were getting in the early seventies that Gacy was, in fact, a very bad man, they still insist he just didn't stand out. And how do you handle a John Wayne Gacy? A once-in-a-lifetime apex predator.

'These people – John Gacy and other mass murderers, or predators, or sexual predators, or whatever they may be – they don't walk around and have horns on their head, or this evil look on their face all the time that would scare anybody away,' retired Des Plaines homicide investigator Michael Albrecht said in 2021. To Albrecht and others who encountered John Wayne Gacy, he just seemed to be an ordinary, working-class guy from the Chicago suburbs. 'I mean, he was basically your guy next door … he was very well-liked and respected,' Albrecht said. 'You know, people think of John Gacy as this big, evil, mean person that had to be scary – but it wasn't like that at all.' The veteran detective had a lot of time to get to know Gacy. As investigators closed in on him during late 1978, Albrecht talked to the chatty killer – a lot. He shared meals with Gacy at local restaurants and bars, even as the detective was determined to put his quarry on ice. 'Guys like Gacy, they're not so easy to recognise in the cold light of day,' Albrecht said. 'You can't be suspicious of everybody that you come in contact with, in your life, but you can't be easy-going, blasé about it either. You're dealing with humans. Humans are not perfect by any means.'

But after Gacy's divorce was finalised and Carole and the two girls moved out of 8213 West Summerdale Avenue, even the neighbours began noticing changes in Gacy. The Oldsmobile would leave or return at all hours. The lights in the house would frequently turn on and off in the hours before dawn. One of Gacy's neighbours may have aurally witnessed much worse. After Gacy's arrest, the woman said that she had heard the chilling sounds of muffled high-pitched screaming, shouting, and crying. The frightening sounds often awakened her and her son in the early morning hours. Those terrible sounds, she told cops, were coming from Gacy's house.

Gacy was well on his way as a rapist in 1972, but murder, now that was something different. Albrecht believes that he was emboldened after the murder of McCoy. 'Well, there was no altered personality or whatever you want to call it. Gacy was very cunning in what he did, he knew exactly what he was doing,' Albrecht said. 'I'm sure after that [the murder of McCoy], Gacy was a little concerned about what was going to happen. But nothing happened, the police didn't come by. Nobody came looking for that kid or associated Gacy with him. And I think that's how it started. Most of his victims were probably kids that had run away from other parts, rural areas, and come to the city. And you could pretty well tell a kid that's walking around in amazement in a large city like Chicago and is also kind of lost. And Gacy had a car that he had a spotlight on, with a red light on it. And he had police identification, some police badges. Then he would start talking to these kids and get them in the car. Eventually, take them back to his house. The first few times, there was small talk, entertainment, drinking, and drugs, and all that stuff before he got into the sexual part of it. Gacy would do his handcuff trick and then what he called the "rope trick" … So, he knew what he was doing.'

Now, in 1976, divorced, living alone and having got away with three murders – John Wayne Gacy was fully committed to the prospect of murder for pleasure. His reign of terror would go unnoticed for two more years until finally, Gacy's own twisted bloodlust became his undoing. But before that happened, he would kill again and again, utterly unfettered by cops, conscience or any semblance of morality.

10

1976

After his conviction in Iowa, one of John Wayne Gacy's most cherished goals was a return to prominence in the worlds of commerce and politics. As well as his penchant for the perverted, he had not lost his interest in politics. Just eight short years ago, Gacy had been a high-flier in Waterloo, and a big hitter with the Jaycees. And he had been considering running for political office in the Cornhusker State when that all came crashing down. In the spring of 1968 when he was arrested for sexually assaulting two teenage boys, Gacy lost his standing in the community, his wife, children and career in one fell swoop. While Gacy did only a short eighteen-month stint in prison before being released on parole, his reputation there had been ruined.

Now, in 1976 and back in Chicago, he wanted that standing and respect from the political community back. Desperately. Oh, there were a few bumps along the way, mostly involving young men and the police but nothing ever came of them. His darkest secrets remained well hidden. Eventually, through his work with the Moose Lodge and his community involvement in Chicago, Gacy came to the attention of local Democratic Party powerbroker, Robert F. Matwick. He was the Dems committee-man for Gacy's Norwood Park community. As a service to the community, Gacy and his young workforce had volunteered to clean up the Democratic Party headquarters. And Gacy's incarnation as Pogo the Clown also reportedly impressed Matwick. The political fixer thought his happy new friend had a big heart. In 1975, Matwick nominated Gacy to the street lighting commission, where he became secretary-treasurer. It was a small step up the ladder in the roiling politics of Chicago, but a step nonetheless.

But behind his façade, Gacy continued paying teen boys he'd picked up in Bughouse Square and Uptown for sex as well as some of his employees. In January 1976, a nine-year-old boy who had been sex trafficked, disappeared from Uptown. Chicago detectives searching for the child kept hearing the name 'John' – supposedly a contractor from the suburbs – from young men around the area. It didn't take long to connect to Gacy. Both his work van and his late-model, black Delta 88 Oldsmobile had P. D. M. Contracting painted on the sides. Investigators were way out of their jurisdiction, but for several weeks they had staked out Gacy's home. The missing boy eventually showed up and the matter was dropped by the Chicago Police Department.

It was another close call for Gacy. That poor young boy hadn't become one of his victims but, by early 1976, Gacy had already killed three times. Those poor boys would turn out to be his cocktail hour of carnage. The main courses, dessert and after-dinner drinks were about to come.

Darrell Samson was eighteen years old when he fell into the clutches of a killer. Born in West Virginia, his parents had been part of the great Appalachian migration north to Chicago and other parts of the industrial heart of America of people looking for work and opportunity. Most simply found more heartache:

squalid tenements, poverty, hunger, indifference – and violence. He lived on the city's South Side and worked at a carpeting company in suburban Libertyville. Darrell was hard-working with dreams well beyond his current situation. It would be his strong work ethic that would kill him.

Darrell went missing on 6 April 1976. His mother Delores would later tell newspapers that her son's sudden disappearance was not like him at all. Darrell was home every night – and now he wasn't. She tried to get the attention of Chicago cops and even called authorities in other states where Darrell may have gone – if, in fact, his disappearance had been voluntary. Cops in the Windy City put the teenager's disappearance down to a favourite answer of the time – Darrell was a runaway.

Delores didn't stop looking for her son. 'Here in Chicago I found myself walking the streets at night looking for him,' his mother said. 'I wore blisters on the bottom of my feet … I burned up four cars trying to find him.'

Four years later, when Gacy was on trial for the murder of her son, Delores appeared in court. Reports recorded: 'Mrs Vance said that he [Darrell] had never been gone from home more than a day or night and that when he didn't return, she informed the police. Shown a picture of her son, she broke down, sobbing heavily.'

When Darrell's remains were found in 1978, the best detectives could piece together of the final hours of his life was that they were spent at the home of John Wayne Gacy. It is likely that Gacy had lured the teen into his house of horrors with the promise of a job. There, Samson was murdered, no doubt having been tortured and raped beforehand. In the volumes of correspondence and media and police interviews, Samson was never mentioned by Gacy.

For years, his resting place was under the floorboards in Gacy's dining room, which he was remodelling at the time. And that is where he was found. When police finally recovered his body, they found a gag stuffed into his mouth.

Now, Gacy had killed four times – and he kept getting away with it. With his marriage to Carole over, he was living alone and he could kill at leisure, feeding his seemingly unquenchable bloodlust. Gacy had murdered in 1972, 1974 and 1975, at a rate slightly lower than one homicide a year. Now, Darrell Samson was dead and six weeks later, Gacy would murder again.

* * * *

The first time Randy Reffett and Sam Stapleton met on the streets of Uptown was probably sometime in 1972 or 1973. Both boys' families had come from the south, looking for something better in Chicago. When they met, Randy was the reigning neighbourhood tough guy and Sam was the new kid on the block. One day the pair scrapped in front of a screaming crowd of kids. The newcomer left the former heavyweight bloodied and sore. They were eleven and twelve years old at the time. But like a lot of fisticuffs between young boys, there was no long-lasting hatred or resentment and the two became friends.

'They never had no grudge,' Randy's brother Clyde told author David Nelson in his excellent book on Gacy's victims, *Boys Enter the House*. Still, Clyde Reffett recalled that the two 'would go at it again, sometimes two, three times the same day.'

On 14 May 1976, John Wayne Gacy returned to one of his favourite hunting grounds in Uptown. There, Randy was walking home from a dental appointment after school. He was last seen by his grandmother that afternoon. Sometime after that, Randy, then fifteen, was approached by the man driving the black late-model Oldsmobile. Hours later, his friend Sam Stapleton, fourteen, disappeared somewhere between his sister's apartment and home.

They were both destined for the crawl space underneath Gacy's home. Like other victims, Randy died with a gag in his mouth causing his asphyxiation. Sam was strangled to death and the two friends were buried alongside each other in the rancid crypt. It was the first time Gacy had killed two boys on the same day, but it would certainly not be the last. The boys were from Uptown and it didn't seem like anyone was going to miss them; at least that's what Gacy thought.

The next victim was a seventeen-year-old from the Lakeview neighbourhood on the city's North Side, near Wrigley Field, named Michael Bonnin. He vanished on 3 June 1976, while travelling from Chicago to Waukegan, forty-seven miles north of Chicago. At the time, Bonnin was working as a carpenter and was refinishing an old jukebox for his uncle. The deadline for completion was the coming weekend. He was en route to meet his uncle when he disappeared.

Somehow, Gacy lured him into his Oldsmobile, and the two then ended up at the home on Summerdale Avenue. Bonnin never made it out of the house alive. Gacy later confessed that he strangled Bonnin with a ligature and buried him under his spare bedroom.

Bonnin's sister is Chicago radio host, comedienne and Democratic Party member of the state legislature, Patti Vasquez. She finally opened up to *Chicago* magazine in 2019 about how his murder had affected her. Vasquez finally felt it was time to honour her brother and herself and reveal the awful truth about her family's tragic history. She said that the slaying has haunted her and her family ever since that terrible day in 1976. She was just four years old when her brother vanished, and seven when his body was identified. For her comedy career, also her subsequent work in radio, she made a conscious decision to change her surname to her mother's maiden name. She also wanted to escape any connection to John Wayne Gacy.

'I knew our name was going to be in the paper again,' she told the magazine. 'I didn't want [the murder] to precede every conversation and interview I gave … It's painful to dive into it … I was four when Mike disappeared, so everything I know about him is more from the experience of my dad trying to find him. What I remember is my dad taking me to police stations with a picture of Mike. It's the same black-and-white picture that you see on the grid of the victims. When he went missing they were in complete shock. It didn't make any sense to them that he was gone. He was seventeen.'

Her brother's murder wasn't much discussed at home after Gacy was arrested. It was only through her own research and time that Vasquez learned the horrific truth. But she does remember Christmas 1978. By this point her brother had been missing for more than two years with no answers in sight.

'I do remember the phone ringing because it was the holiday season. My mom was doing the dishes and answered the phone. It was a Saturday and my dad was still sleeping. He was a cab driver, so he had weird hours,' Vasquez said. 'I remember my mom waking up my dad and saying, "It's about Mike." They had found Mike's fishing licence in Gacy's belongings. This was just a few days after he was arrested, and they had a definite I. D. on 6 January, through dental records. How do you talk to a seven-year-old [about that] when she's still waiting for Santa? I also think [my parents] were in shock – unable to process what was happening. So, I didn't know a lot when I was little.'

Even though she didn't live far from the notorious house of death on Summerdale Avenue, she never saw it until high school when Vasquez and some friends took a cruise past in a car. Her friends had no idea that her big brother had been a victim of John Wayne Gacy.

Vasquez said in 2019 that the disappearance of their son left her parents heartbroken. 'It destroyed my father, not knowing.

I've asked my mom, but it wasn't something my dad and I really discussed. The only thing I would get from my dad was when he was at his lowest. He would wonder if, had he been a better father, things would be different.'

The details of her brother's death quite literally killed their parents, Vasquez said. His mother Shirley died less than fifteen years after her teenage boy.

'My dad was sixty-eight when he died in 2001. I think that Shirley was in her late fifties. My dad struggled with alcoholism after Mike died. He stopped drinking for the last twelve years of his life, but he was also a heavy smoker because of the anxiety,' she said. 'It certainly took its toll. When he drank he would call Shirley crying. Because our apartment was so small, I could hear everything he was saying. He would beg her for forgiveness and say, "I'm the one who should have died, not Mike. If I'd been a better father, if I had been there." I do remember one time, my mom said it was worse knowing how he died than thinking he was never coming home. It was worse knowing how he died.' The horror was incomprehensible.

Gacy's crime and her brother's murder have resurfaced in terrible coincidences for Vasquez.

'I met this guy, Steve, who told me he went to high school with one of the victims. When he said he went to Luther North, I asked him what was the victim's name and he said Mike,' she said. 'I told him Mike was my brother and asked what can he tell me about him. He said he had a great laugh, these great blue eyes and strawberry-blond hair. He also said he was a great baseball player. I didn't know that.'

By that summer of 1976, the Gacy murder machine was rolling at full-tilt. He had murdered four boys in less than four months and showed no signs of slowing. The third-largest city in America had a serial killer on its hands and nobody realised – the public was completely in the dark and so were the cops.

'Gacy was very sure of himself. I mean, he'd been doing this since 1972. He put the first one in the crawl space and he put concrete over that one,' retired detective Mike Albrecht said. 'I'm sure he was nervous for a while after that about what was going to happen, and nothing happened. And then he continued, and he probably thought he was well protected, as far as he thought, because he had this great scheme going on.'

William 'Billy' Carroll was sixteen years old and known as a bit of a hell-raiser around Uptown. Billy had grown up on the streets and had been in trouble ever since his parents could remember. When he was nine years old he was sent to a juvenile home for stealing a woman's purse. Two years later, when he was eleven, he was caught with a gun.

His parents, like Reffett and Stapleton's, came from Appalachia – eastern Tennessee, to be precise. Billy knew the drill of poverty and the streets. When his remains were discovered and his family got the bad news, more than two years after he had disappeared, sadly it did not come as a surprise.

'I expected it because I knew his habits so well,' his dad William Huey Carroll told the *Chicago Tribune*. 'It's hard for me to accept, but a fact's a fact.' His tearful dad described his son as handsome, athletic – and a troublemaker. 'He liked money. He never actually picked my pocket or anything, but he was kind of clever and sometimes I'd let him talk me out of my money.' Once, his father said, the boy reached out the window of a slow-moving elevated train and snatched a woman's purse containing 'three or four hundred dollars' as she stood on the train platform.

On the night he vanished, Billy promised he'd be home 'in about an hour'. His dad watched him leave with three or four other boys in a car.

Marianne Rogers, who was friends with Billy, said he was a good weightlifter and boxer, but 'liked cars and reefers'. She said she had a premonition of the night her friend's body was discovered.

'I dreamt about him [Billy] until about a week before the Gacy case broke,' she told reporters as she trembled. 'It would be night-time and there would be lots of lights and lots of concrete.'

Uptown was known for the prevalence of 'chicken hawks' – men who desired sex with underage boys. They would cruise the streets eyeing what might be available. In the summer, they would drive past the neighbourhood public pool, eyeing innocent young bodies. In those times and in that place, people did what they had to survive – both the hustlers and their agents, like Billy Carroll. Billy would reportedly arrange hookups between older men and teen boys for sex and would take a commission.

On 13 June 1976, Billy Carroll vanished off the streets of Uptown. In the poverty-stricken neighbourhood, it was not unusual for people to go missing. People came and went all the time, whether it was back home to Appalachia or in pursuit of greener pastures, it was part of the transient nature of the area. And for a kid like Billy, this was not unusual at all. Still, ten days after he had vanished, his parents reported him missing.

The details are vague about whether he was snatched off the streets by Gacy, or perhaps went with him willingly. One thing is clear: within hours Billy had been tortured, raped and murdered by a homicidal maniac. And the city did not utter a peep nor shed a tear for Billy Carroll.

Another boy had disappeared. But even if cops had pieced together the unfolding horror, there were obstacles. The young men and boys had met their killer in the inner city and were then murdered in the far suburbs, a completely different police jurisdiction. Today, it is likely that the pieces of the puzzle would have been put together much more quickly because of advances in technology and better police co-ordination and co-operation. Numerous lives would probably have been saved.

'Other than a parent making a missing-person report of a juvenile or another person, [we'd take] as much information as we could and we'd put it out to other departments,' retired Cook County Sheriff's investigator Phil Bettiker said. 'But as far as an active pursuit of trying to locate them, there wasn't that much done, unless they were a fragile youth or something like that. But for the ages of most of the Gacy victims, if they're runaways, they're runaways. We try to locate them … but there wasn't an awful lot we could do.'

That bicentennial summer in America, John Wayne Gacy was in a murdering mood. It was as if, when Carole left, the floodgates to horror had opened. Between 3 June and 6 August 1976, Gacy murdered at least five young men. After murdering Michael Bonnin and Billy Carroll, on 5 August 1976, Gacy got his clutches on the sixteen-year-old Minnesota farm boy, Jimmie Haakenson.

It's likely Gacy picked Jimmie up from the Greyhound Bus Terminal with the offer of work and a solid meal. Jimmie died of suffocation and his body was found beneath the remains of seventeen-year-old Bensenville youth, Rick Johnston, who had last been seen alive on 6 August.

Johnston lived in the suburbs and was, by all accounts, a typical teenager. On that night, he was going into the city to attend a concert in Uptown, at the famed Aragon Ballroom. That night, hard-rocking girl group The Runaways, starring Joan Jett, and groovy California band, Spirit, were on the double bill. Rick planned to attend the show by himself and then call his mother afterwards for a ride. That phone call never came.

'Rick Johnston – he was alone only because he had gone to a concert at the Aragon. His mom had dropped him off. He was supposed to call her to pick him up but she never heard from him,' Cook County Sheriff Tom Dart said in 2017.

Gacy murdered once more during the heady summer of 1976. The fifth victim was an adult male, around twenty-five years old with what appeared to be bad teeth. Nearly fifty years later, he remains one of Gacy's unidentified victims.

Gacy and his vile deeds have stretched across decades in a manner in which few other modern horrors have. Any new information in the John Wayne Gacy case triggers a fresh batch of headlines, news reports, documentaries and speculation. His deeds were evil on a monumental scale.

The families of his victims still endure uninvited visits from Gacy, even though he was executed in 1994. Patti Vasquez thinks of her tragic brother daily. There is no end in sight for her or any of the others whose hearts were shattered by Gacy's murderous appetite.

'He [Michael] would be sixty now. His friend that went to school with him, Steve … every time I see him, I cry, because he was the same age as my brother,' Vasquez told *Chicago* magazine. 'He makes me happy, but he makes me cry. I look at him and think this is how Mike would have aged. I'd get so greedy with his time. Every time I hug him, I don't want to let go, because he's the closest thing I have to Mike.'

'I read somewhere that this [the Gacy murders] will hurt a hundred years of people. A publisher said they wanted [my book],' Vasquez said. But the book is still unwritten because there was one crucial question from the publisher that Vasquez could not answer: 'How does it end?'

11

The Me Decade

By August 1976, John Wayne Gacy was getting good at murder. He now had his routine down pat: the hunt, the capture, the torture, the rape, the killing and finally, the disposal of his prey. And he was doing it while holding neighbourhood barbecues, entertaining sick children as a clown, being a good neighbour and building his contracting business.

The victims were young men and boys he knew and random strangers he'd picked up from the seedy Greyhound Bus Terminal, the gay mecca of Bughouse Square or off the streets of down-at-heel Uptown. He would offer jobs, booze, money or drugs to get the boys into his black Delta 88 Oldsmobile. Most of the time, he didn't even have to use force to get the boys into his car. He frequently used his bogus sheriff's badge and would simply tell the kids that he was a cop. Some of them thought it was sex he wanted – and they were right but he also wanted much, much more.

Usually it was a single victim but Gacy had committed the first of what he called 'doubles' – when he would murder two victims in the same evening at his home – the night he murdered Randy Reffett and Sam Stapleton.

Once he had the boys inside the modest bungalow, he would ply his victims with liquor and drugs. He would work to gain their trust. And why shouldn't they trust him? He was affable, jolly, generous and understanding. At some point, the thirty-four-year-old would pull out a pair of toy handcuffs, and maybe show them his 'handcuff trick'. Gacy would cuff his own hands behind his back then would clandestinely release himself with a hidden key. 'You want to know how it's done?' Gacy would ask his victims? He would then put them in cuffs. Once they were secured, Gacy would snicker at his victim: 'The trick is, you have to have the key.' And the suddenly frightened quarry would start to panic as they realised their mistake and struggled to get free. Gacy would then immobilise his prisoner's legs by attaching their ankles to a two-by-four with handcuffs attached at each end. With his victim restrained, he would then rape and torture the captive.

According to later interviews with the killer, he would begin by sitting on or straddling his victim's chest and would then force the victim to perform oral sex. Then would come the torture portion of the evening. He would burn the boys with cigars. He would make them imitate a horse as he sat on their backs and pulled hard on some sort of makeshift reins that went around their necks. The killer would violate his captives with dildos, pill bottles and inflict other indignities. He forced many to crawl to his bathroom where he would partially drown them in the tub before reviving them. He would then repeat his macabre ritual of rape, torture then partial drowning … again and again.

And he would taunt the victims as they screamed in agony. If the victim begged to be released from the misery with a merciful death? Gacy would simply laugh, telling them that he would kill them when he wanted to. Death typically came with Gacy placing a tourniquet made of rope around his young victim's neck, then tightening the rope with a hammer handle until they passed out and then eventually stopped breathing. He called this the 'rope trick'. And once more, he couldn't resist humiliating his victims. After hours of torture, he would inform them: 'This is the last trick.'

What Gacy liked, and was sexually turned on by, was when his victim convulsed for an hour or two before expiring. Other victims died by asphyxiation from the cloth gags, socks and underwear stuffed into their throats. Most of the victims perished between the hours of three and six a.m. And when they were finally dead, their agonising final hours on this mortal coil at an end, Gacy would stash their bodies under his bed. Then, exhilarated and exhausted, he would fall asleep on the bed above.

Often he'd leave the corpses there for a day or so. After they had been killed, Gacy sometimes took victims' remains to his garage where he performed a bizarre DIY embalming process before relegating them to the crawl space crypt. And like Samuel L. Jackson's Bible-quoting hitman in Quentin Tarantino's box-office smash-hit crime thriller, *Pulp Fiction*, Gacy also turned to the good book. He would read part of Psalm 23 to his doomed captives:

The Lord is my shepherd, I shall not be in want.
He makes me lie down in green pastures, he leads me
    beside quiet waters.
He restores my soul. He guides me in paths of
    righteousness for his name's sake.
Even though I walk through the valley of the shadow of
    death, I will fear no evil, for you are with me; your rod and
    your staff, they comfort me.

After burying their lifeless bodies in the crawl space underneath the house, he would then pour quicklime over the corpses to speed up the decomposition process and to temper the stench that even friends of the killer had noted by now.

Gacy's death count now stood at ten as the summer of 1976 turned into autumn. And he added two more kills sometime between August and October. These two victims have never been identified, and investigators only managed to approximate their time of death from when they were buried in the crawl space.

The first unidentified victim was between eighteen to twenty-two years old and was suffering from dental problems at the time of his death. The second victim was also a white male (Gacy's preference), and he was between the ages of fifteen and twenty-four at the time he was murdered.

* * * *

Gacy later admitted that he was patterning his methods after another serial killer: Houston's Dean Corll – known as 'The Candy Man'. Corll's family owned a confectionery factory in Houston Heights – and he was known for sharing treats with local children. Between 1970 and 1973, Corll raped, tortured and murdered approximately twenty-eight teenage boys and young men. Most of the murders occurred in Houston, Texas, while others occurred in nearby Pasadena.

Corll – born in Fort Wayne, Indiana, in 1939 – had two teen accomplices who aided him in his twisted enterprise by sourcing victims. The wicked extent of Corll's evil was only revealed when one of the teens finally broke and sprayed a slew of bullets into the Candy Man.

When his crimes were uncovered, Corll was thought to be the most prolific serial murderer in the United States. Like Gacy, Corll would target vulnerable and often impoverished young victims and offer them drugs, booze or a ride in his car. Then the boys would be restrained by force – or deception – tortured, raped and murdered. The Candy Man would then strangle the luckless teens, or shoot them to death with a .22-calibre Saturday Night Special. Afterwards, Corll and his accomplices would dispose of the bodies. At least seventeen victims were buried in a rented boat shed, while others were planted in the woods, on beaches. It didn't matter to Corll – they were dead.

As in Chicago, Houston police thought the missing boys were simply runaways, a familiar product of their times. But there were more chilling similarities between Gacy and Corll. Gacy trolled rundown Uptown while Corll hunted in Houston Heights – a poor-white neighbourhood where money was always tight. Most of his victims were also in their mid-teens. Like Gacy after him, Corll would also trick his stupefied, prospective victims into trying out his handcuffs. Sometimes, he simply physically forced them into doing what he desired.

Once his victims were subdued, the boys were stripped naked then tied to Corll's bed or a do-it-yourself plywood torture board hung against the wall. Then, they would be raped, beaten and tortured – often over a period of days. Once Corll killed them they were wrapped in plastic sheeting and dumped.

A 2021 documentary called *The Clown and The Candyman* posits that the two serial killers were part of a larger, nationwide ring of paedophiles. 'They operated for so long in big cities in plain sight and nobody noticed,' director Jacqueline Bynon told Sky News. 'The interesting thing looking back from our perspective today is, nobody cared about boys then. They called them runaways. They didn't matter … In one high school – in one little area – eleven boys were missing and nobody noticed. Remember in the early seventies, it was just after *Easy Rider*; doing your own thing; marijuana – the counterculture was there. Boys were doing that. And some of them were going to the Vietnam War and not coming back.

'So when the seats were empty in the classroom, nobody noticed. If they had been girls, as one cop said to me, this would have been different. If a girl had gone missing, they would have put a lot of time into it.'

John Wayne Gacy was also killing boys and no one seemed to care. By late October 1976, he was ready to kill again. Whether it was a conscious decision to make it a 'double', only John Gacy knew. On 24 October 1976, Michael Marino, fourteen, and his best friend, Kenneth 'Kenny' Parker, sixteen, made plans to go hang out at an Uptown arcade. Neither boy knew that the popular pinball arcade in the neighbourhood was a favourite trolling spot for Gacy.

Marino left the house he shared with his mother Sherry and two sisters. 'It was a Sunday, at two o'clock in the afternoon,' his mother told *People* magazine in 2014. 'He made me a sandwich and said, "Mom, I'm going to the game room." Then he kissed me on my cheek and went off. I told him to be back by six because we were going to go to the movies that night. Michael was very punctual. If he said he'd be there at six, he'd be there at six. So I was very worried when it got to be 6.15 and he wasn't home.'

When Michael didn't return home, Marino says, she 'went from worried to frantic.' Around nine or ten p.m., she began calling the cops. In those days, a person had to have been missing for twenty-four hours before authorities would act.

Eventually, the police told her Michael had probably run away. 'They said it's what teenage boys do. I said, "You don't know my son,"' Sherry recalled. Sherry said her son was a 'very kind, very good' kid who never got into trouble. He was a talented drummer whose favorite song was Led Zeppelin's iconic 'Stairway to Heaven'.

Michael became Victim No. 14. Sherry never believed her son had run away and would wage a decades-long battle with cops and bureaucrats trying to get answers. In her mind's eye, there were too many inconsistencies. And so, the gutsy mom began a lonely crusade to find her son, pounding the mean streets of Chicago looking for answers. She put up missing posters and went into drug dens, fearing her boy had fallen into the area's thriving dope subculture.

'I would push my way through doorways where people were getting high. I would say, "I'm looking for my son,"' she said. She sank almost every penny she had into private detectives.

Even after the killer was arrested she never thought her son might be one of his victims. 'When I saw it, I thought, "Oh my God. Those poor parents. I feel so bad for them,"' she said. 'I never thought Michael was ever a victim.'

According to reports, the two boys were last seen in front of a Clark Street restaurant on the North Side. Cops later said the two were strangled and buried together underneath Gacy's house.

Not satisfied with his second 'double', Gacy apparently got the itch to kill once more, just two days later. This time, the victim was construction worker William Bundy, who may have done work for Gacy's P. D. M. Contracting. The nineteen-year-old Chicago native vanished after informing his family that he was going to a party on the night of 26 October 1976. It would take thirty-five years to finally identify his remains that were buried beneath Gacy's master bedroom.

Francis Wayne Alexander, another victim that was identified as part of the efforts started by Cook County Sheriff Tom Dart in 2011, was murdered some time between November and December 1976. His remains had been buried in the crawl space beneath the room Gacy used as an office for his construction business. Bundy would finally be identified in 2021.

If John Wayne Gacy was brimming with confidence over his ability to escape detection and scrutiny over his murderous activities, he had good reason. Although his name appeared far too often in police notebooks for alleged sexual offences, no one in law enforcement was connecting the dots on the missing men and boys of Uptown. Nor did the missing boys from the more respectable, middle-class suburbs move the needle. It was just boys being boys, cops would tell their alarmed parents.

By the start of December 1976, John Wayne Gacy had killed thirteen times that year, at last untethered by any semblance of restraint. Add to that murders in 1972, 1974 and 1975 and that made sixteen homicides. Before the year was out, Gacy would kill one more time before the calendar flipped over to 1977 when the slaughter would begin anew. Gregory Godzik would be the final known victim of 1976.

The seventeen-year-old Taft High School student came from a stable home environment with two hard-working and dedicated parents. He needed money to get parts for his car and he found work with Gacy's P. D. M. Contracting. 'All Greg said was that he [Gacy] was a very nice man to work for,' his mother Eugenia Godzik told the *Chicago Tribune* in 1979.

Godzik and another teen were hired to 'dig trenches for some kind of (drain) tiles' in the crawl space under Gacy's Summerdale Avenue home. 'Greg bragged about the job saying it was the best job he ever had,' friend, Tim Best told the *Tribune*. What the young man didn't know was that he was digging his own grave.

On 12 December 1976, Godzik told his parents he was going to a party with his girlfriend. And that was the last they heard of him. His girlfriend said that her sweetheart had dropped her off and left. She assumed he was going home. Greg's abandoned car was found in nearby Niles, Illinois by friends. And it was also his friends who told the cops he worked for a man named John Wayne Gacy. Godzik's parents and his older sister, Eugenia, called Gacy hoping the respected contractor might be able to shed some light on the boy's disappearance. Did Gacy know anything about the teenager's vanishing act?

Gacy told the boy's family that Greg had told him that he planned to run away from home. It was something he had talked about, the contractor helpfully offered. In fact, he told the frantic Godzik clan, he had received a message from the teenager on his answering machine after he had vanished. When the family asked to hear it, Gacy told them he was sorry, he must have erased it.

Godzik's family hired private detectives in a desperate effort to find Greg. There were some flickers of hope, but mostly the results lead to more heartache for the devastated family. Years later, when cops were tearing apart every nail and board in Gacy's bungalow, they found Greg Godzik's wallet in the crawl space. On that late December day in 1978, Greg's friend Tim Best stood outside Gacy's house with hundreds of other onlookers and concerned friends and families of the other missing boys. He told the *Sun-Times* he was terrified 'they'd find Greg in there'.

'I just became frantic. Of course, I'm hoping it's not Greg,' his mom told the *Tribune*.

P. D. M. was a beehive of activity for Gacy. And a place where he had easy access to young men who he would often proposition for sex. He would offer his chosen boys use of his vehicles, money or promotions – in exchange for sex. And if a boy was so inclined, Gacy said he had access to weapons. Some of his sexual innuendo and suggestive remarks missed the mark with his teenage male workforce. But if his overtures weren't received how he hoped, he would walk them back – tell the boys he was just kidding.

In 1973, he'd had another brush with discovery when he took one of his teen employees on a jolly to Florida. The purpose of the trip was to check out a property the contractor had just purchased. But on the first night in Florida, Gacy was Gacy and he raped the worker in his hotel room. No hard feelings, right? Wrong.

After they returned to Chicago, the boy drove to Gacy's house and beat him senseless in his front yard. Wily Gacy told his then wife, Carole, that the kid wanted money. He wasn't going to give it to the boy because he had done a lousy job painting something or the other.

Then there had been the incident with fifteen-year-old Anthony Antonucci. In May 1975, Gacy had hired the teen to help him and the P. D. M. crew clean up the Democratic Party headquarters. This was very important to Gacy as he continued to rebuild his tarnished political brand.

Two months later, Antonucci injured his foot while working for Gacy. His boss – armed with a bottle of wine – went to the youth's home where they polished off the vino and watched a porn movie. Again, Gacy pulled the 'handcuff trick', wrestling the boy to the floor before cuffing his victim's hands behind his back. What the older man didn't realise was that one of the cuffs was loose and Antonucci – a champion high-school wrestler – managed to free his arm while his tormentor was out of the room. When Gacy returned, Antonucci pounced on him, wrestling the predator to the floor before turning the tables and cuffing him.

Gacy told the wrestler he'd passed the test: 'Not only are you the only one who got out of the cuffs, you got them on me.' Unsure what else to do, and unaware that he'd just had a narrow escape, Antonucci released Gacy and he left. Antonucci had avoided becoming another victim of Gacy.

There was another young man who lived to tell the tale of his encounter with the killer. On 26 July 1976, John Wayne Gacy picked up eighteen-year-old hitch-hiker David Cram. Gacy offered him a job with P. D. M. and he commenced working for him that night.

In need of a place to stay, on 21 August 1976, Cram moved into Gacy's house of horrors. The next day, the two men were boozing to celebrate Cram's nineteenth birthday. Gacy even dressed as Pogo the Clown. Like Anthony Antonucci before him, Gacy tricked Cram into putting on handcuffs. The teenager's wrists were cuffed in front, unusually, rather than behind. Gacy reportedly swung Cram around while still holding the chain linking the two cuffs. Gacy had decided he would rape the boy and told him so.

Cram, however, was as wily as Gacy. He kicked his thirty-four-year-old boss in the face and freed himself. He didn't move out though and, one month later, his boss tried it on again. The teenager woke up with Gacy standing at his bedroom door. Again, the predator's intention was to rape the boy.

Cram later told reporters that Gacy said: 'Dave, you really don't know who I am. Maybe it would be good if you give me what I want.'

The teen resisted and once more got the better of Gacy, who then left his room, sneering, 'You ain't no fun.' Cram now recognised it was time to go and he left the house and P. D. M. in October, although he continued to work periodically for Gacy.

At the end of 1976, still sailing under the radar, Gacy was a seasoned serial killer and he hoped the new year of 1977 would be just as fruitful.

12

1977

By the time the clock struck 12.01 a.m. on 1 January 1977, John Wayne Gacy had killed at least eighteen times. He was no longer an amateur, but a practised predator. Best of all for Gacy, the cops still weren't onto him. There had been some minor run-ins with the law, but happily they had stopped at Gacy's door, when the respected businessman would innocently tell law enforcement, 'Gee, I'd like to help you, but ...'

When the parents of a number of his teen P. D. M. workers who had disappeared begged investigators to take a closer look at this Mr. Gacy, they were blown off. And why not? Gacy was heavily involved in the community as a member of the Moose Lodge, a Democratic Party precinct captain and as the big-hearted Pogo the Clown. It seemed as if the gregarious contractor was friends with everyone who mattered – he couldn't possibly be involved with any disappearances.

At the end of 1976, the United States had a new president in the wings in former Georgia governor and peanut farmer Jimmy Carter, who, for a brief moment, brought hope to a country still reeling from Richard Nixon's Watergate, the energy crisis and Vietnam. That January, the Oakland Raiders defeated the Minnesota Vikings 32–14 in Super Bowl XI in Pasadena, California; snow fell in Miami; and the United States resumed executions, with the death of killer Gary Gilmore by firing squad in Utah.

On 20 January 1977, Carter was sworn in as the thirty-ninth president of the United States, with Walter Mondale as vice-president. It was also the date on which John Wayne Gacy began killing again, after a six-week break over Christmas and the holidays.

John Szyc was nineteen years old. He was the middle child of a happy family of five. His parents, Richard and Rosemarie Szyc, never had any problems with the boy. They said Johnny was a natural comedian who knew how to make people laugh. He even wrote and filmed short, homemade comedies that he shared with family and friends. John Szyc's ambition was to work in the entertainment business, maybe as a cameraman. That was his dream, anyway. He had just moved out of his parents' house in suburban Des Plaines and was now renting an apartment in Chicago. On 20 January 1977, Szyc was back on his old turf in the suburbs enquiring about selling his 1971 Plymouth Satellite. The buyer was a man named John Wayne Gacy.

According to the book *The Man Who Killed Boys* by Clifford L. Linedecker, Szyc had known two of the killer's previous victims, Greg Godzik and Johnny Butkovich. The author adds that he had also 'been an acquaintance of John Gacy, although he hadn't worked for P. D. M. Contractors'.

When they couldn't get hold of their boy, the Szycs raised the alarm with the police. Not long after the teenager disappeared, another teen was picked up by cops driving Szyc's Plymouth Satellite. He was trying to pull a 'gas-and-dash' (avoiding paying after filling up the gas tank), officers said. The driver was young Gacy employee and acolyte Michael Rossi. His boss had sold him the car for $300. 'Talk to the man I work for,' Rossi told cops. 'He can explain everything.'

'Why, yes,' smooth John Wayne Gacy told officers, Johnny Szyc had sold him the Plymouth. Anything else? No?

And that was that.

Yet again the cops had missed vital information. They never checked the car's paperwork. If they had, they would have seen that the title had been signed eighteen days after John Szyc vanished and that the signature on the paper did not match the young man's.

Gacy later told detectives that he had strangled Szyc to death in his spare bedroom.

Their son's disappearance haunted Richard and Rosemarie Szyc for years. Like many other parents and siblings of Gacy victims, their lives were haunted by the horrors their boy had endured. 'I have nightmares. I go crazy,' Richard Szyc said in 1994. 'Sometimes I think about walking into this lake, about suicide. I dream as if I'm next, the man is strangling me.'

Sometime during the winter of 1977, Gacy killed again. Little is known about the victim or the circumstances of his murder. He remains unidentified. He was a white male between the ages of twenty-two and thirty-three. His only identifying marker was a key fob with the name 'Greg' written on it.

After the close call with Johnny Szyc's car, a more prudent, less arrogant serial killer may have paused his killing spree for a few months. And Gacy was, if nothing else, cautious. But time and again, these close calls had amounted to nothing. The cops just weren't piecing it together. The police were hindered by a lack of technology, many different jurisdictions and old-fashioned laziness.

There was also the matter of who many of the missing boys were: poverty-stricken hustlers from the poor side of town – easy to write-off as runaways. They were the 'missing missing' that Arntfield refers to. But what about the boys from the suburbs? Szyc, Godzik and Butkovich weren't street kids, and their parents were being very vocal in their search to establish their whereabouts. Even when Gacy's name had been linked to some of the missing boys, connections still weren't made. The Teflon John seemed to continue his run of luck.

On 15 March 1977, two days before his thirty-fifth birthday, John Wayne Gacy struck again.

Jon Prestidge was a twenty-year-old from Kalamazoo, Michigan. His parents lived just outside that city and sometimes he reportedly stayed with his father in his trailer. After graduating from high school, Prestidge attended community college where he took courses related to healthcare professions. To put himself through college, Prestidge worked at a nearby motel, where pals said he sometimes clashed with management.

But like a lot of other young men, Prestidge was restless and, in early March, he headed to Chicago as part of a planned skiing trip to Colorado. He stayed with an older friend named Roger Sahs. On the final night of his life, Sahs drove his young guest to the barber for a haircut. Coffee followed at the Oak Tree diner. According to the *Chicago Sun-Times*, Prestidge then made a tragic decision: He told Sahs he needed money. Could his friend drop him off at Bughouse Square? He knew that the near North Side area was notorious for male prostitution. But Prestidge did not return from his hustling expedition. He could not have know that, among the frequent fliers of Bughouse Square, was a contractor from Des Plaines.

At first, when his friend failed to return, Sahs thought he must have returned to his family in Kalamazoo. When he called them, he was alarmed to discover that Prestidge was not there. Nor had their adventurous son contacted them. Sahs even placed a missing ad in the city's *Gay Life* magazine but there was no sign of Prestidge. Fate had delivered him into the clutches of a monster. His body was later found in the crawl space under Gacy's home.

Gacy then killed again some time in the spring or early summer of 1977. The victim was a white male between the ages of seventeen and twenty-one. Little is known about how he died as he is among a handful of victims still known only to God, but at some point his left clavicle had been broken.

Even decades later, detectives who worked on the Gacy case fell neatly into two camps. The first believed that the thirty-three victims the Killer Clown claimed were the entirety of his depraved handiwork. However, a second group has long believed that Gacy – who was remarkably well travelled for a man in the 1970s – went on killing expeditions outside his normal hunting grounds. Was this the reason that at times, his murderous rampage in Chicago slowed down? Certainly, he was responsible for less carnage in 1977 than in the previous year. But why?

In the spring of 1977, Gacy took a long break from his murderous frenzy. Around this time, he was trying to woo another woman in an attempt at normalcy. They got engaged, but it was quickly called off. The day after the Fourth of July holiday in Chicago was a summer scorcher. And something stirred in Gacy; it was time, once again, to rape, torture and kill another young man.

Matthew Bowman was eighteen years old, lived in the outer suburbs and was, according to his brother-in-law, 'just looking for a job, that's all'. On 5 July 1977, his mother dropped him off at the train station to catch a commuter-liner to Harwood Heights, where he had a date in court for an unpaid parking ticket. She never saw her son again. His living situation had complicated. He had, his mother thought, been moving back and forth from his sister and brother-in-law's home in Crystal Lake and her home. But there was a twist: Crystal Lake cops said his sister hadn't even moved into her house when Bowman vanished. What is known is that the family had once lived in the Chicago suburb of Harwood Heights – not far from John Wayne Gacy's home on Summerdale Avenue in Norwood Park.

Bowman's mother had tried to report her son's disappearance to the Chicago Police Department. Cops in the Windy City told her to contact the Crystal Lake cops since he was listed as a local resident. Meanwhile, Crystal Lake Police refused to accept the report because the teen lived outside city limits: not our problem.

When cops later found his body under Gacy's abode, the rope which had been used to strangle Bowman was still around his neck.

Bizarrely, John Wayne Gacy cooled his jets during the later summer of 1977, a time when 'I'm Your Boogie Man' by KC and the Sunshine Band, 'Gonna Fly Now', the theme from *Rocky*, and sugary-sweet Shaun Cassidy hit number one with 'Da Doo Ron Ron'. The first instalment of the *Star Wars* saga had made its debut in late May and ruled the box office throughout the summer. The next highest-grossing movie was the Nick Nolte and Jacqueline Bisset thriller *The Deep*. That summer, neither of the city's two baseball teams, the Chicago White Sox and the Chicago Cubs were anywhere near contention. Chicago would have to wait until 2005 for a World Series title when the Sox would go all the way. As for Gacy, he waited two months to resume his murder spree.

Robert Gilroy, eighteen years old, lived just four blocks away from the corpulent killer. On 15 September 1977, the talented equestrian was heading to the stables when he disappeared. Gilroy was different from many of the other missing boys. For starters, his father, Sergeant Robert Gilroy Sr. was a Chicago cop who wasn't going to let matters lie. The police report on Robert Gilroy's disappearance was forty-four pages long, punctuated by twenty follow-up probes. When his boy disappeared, Gilroy began his own investigation and gave the local cops everything he found out.

Gilroy Jr. was last seen around six p.m. on the day he disappeared. He told his parents he was going for a horse riding lesson. But it later emerged that the teenager hadn't attended his lessons at Blue Ribbon Riding Center in weeks. His family had actually considered for a short time the possibility that Gilroy Jr. might have run away. Gilroy Jr. had been slated to attend a special class at the Potomac Horse Center in Maryland on 29 September, but the boy never showed up. His dad reported him missing on 27 September – two weeks after he was last seen by his family.

On 6 November 1977, someone told the increasingly worried father he may have seen the boy entering a posh apartment building on the city's ritzy Gold Coast. His father also discovered that his son had frequented the area of Clark Street and the Diversey Parkway. It was one of Gacy's favourite areas to troll. But despite his investigation, he didn't link the boy to John Wayne Gacy either.

Robert Gilroy Jr. was one of the first of Gacy's victims to be identified. Cops never discovered whether the victim knew his killer or had any previous interactions with him. His autopsy said the boy had been asphyxiated by a piece of cloth crammed down his throat.

After the murder of Robert Gilroy, the autumn of 1977 would see a reanimated John Wayne Gacy kill four more times.

John Mowery had just wrapped up a hitch in the United States Marine Corps and was studying to be an accountant. Like many others, the nineteen-year-old had gone to Gacy's house to enquire about a job. That was on 25 September 1977, and he never left.

When what happened to her son was finally revealed, it tortured his mother for years. She was haunted by what his final hours must have been like. 'God knows. Did he bury them alive?' Dolores Nieder wondered. 'Losing a child is just so horrible, but losing a child the way my son, Johnny, died is just terrible – it's too much to cope with.' And Dolores Nieder tragically knew what she was talking about. Five years before her son disappeared, his older sister had been murdered in an unrelated incident.

A little more than three weeks after John Mowery disappeared, Russell Nelson, a twenty-two-year-old University of Minnesota architecture student also vanished. Nelson had travelled to Chicago with friend Robert Young in his van. The journey was going to be a bit of a road trip with stops in Toronto, New England and then on to sunny Florida.

It was Young who told Nelson about a Chicago contractor who would give the two men work. On the night of 17 October 1977, Nelson and Young had decided to go out dancing at a disco in the area now known as Boystown. Nelson was an accomplished dancer and had even won a number of competitions in his native Minnesota. The pair were outside a watering hole called Crystal's Blinkers on Broadway Avenue when Nelson suddenly vanished into the ether of the autumn night.

At the age of sixteen, Robert Winch of Kalamazoo, Michigan – like Jon Prestidge – had been in and out of foster homes and was now living in Chicago. Winch's father, David, was a physics professor at Kalamazoo College. The boy had been reported missing on 11 November 1977. Robert had been in and out of trouble, and his family – he had a sister and four brothers – said he had recently run away from his current Michigan foster home.

His remains were later discovered in Gacy's crawl space. How he ended up encountering the killer remains a mystery. Once more, it seemed as though Gacy had firmly established his footing. It didn't seem as though anything – let alone the cops – could stop him. A little more than a week after he murdered Winch, John Wayne Gacy would kill again.

This time the victim was twenty-year-old Tommy Boling Jr. Boling wasn't Gacy's typical victim. He was married and already a father. At the time of his 18 November 1977 disappearance, he had been living with his wife Jolli and son Timmie in an apartment on the North Side. Family members told reporters that he had struggled with drugs. He would eventually be identified through his wedding ring, dental charts and a distinctive tiger's-eye belt buckle. Additionally, there were markings on his bones which were caused by a past accident from which he eventually healed. An autopsy would later show that Boling had been strangled to death.

Gacy was not ready to wrap it up for a Christmas break in 1977. David Talsma was another United States marine. The nineteen-year-old Chicago native had told his mother he was going to a rock concert in Hammond, Indiana, on 9 December 1977. She never saw him again.

His father, Peter, had reported him missing on 14 December. Talsma's body was discovered under the crawl space after everything came crashing down on Gacy just over a year later. Cops said Talsma's remains were identified through X-rays which had been taken of his left arm after a previous accident. He would be identified by his father on what would have been his twenty-first birthday.

John Wayne Gacy had managed to get through 1977 without being caught and it didn't appear that police were getting any closer to catching him. While he still had interactions with law enforcement that were no doubt sweat-inducing, no one categorically linked the missing boys to the suburban contractor. Cops would later be hammered on how they could have missed Gacy. How could they have failed to connect the dots? And how many opportunities had they missed that could have stopped the carnage?

Albrecht notes the fact that Gacy was 'popular' in his neighbourhood and he had some powerful political and police pals who might not like it if it looked like their friend was being harassed.

Journalist David Nelson told A&E in 2021 that the killer was woven into the lives of his victims. And that made killing easier. 'One thing that surprised me is that Gacy was a component in many of their lives before they were murdered,' he said. 'A lot of the boys mentioned knowing this contractor who paid really well, and some were employed by him. Some of the victims were involved in sex work, and Gacy was someone coming into their circle … In many instances, these were not chance encounters. He was a figure in their lives for a period of time – as long as several weeks or months before their murders. Yet the cops never looked into him as hard as they could have.' The author noted that it wasn't like Gacy was an unknown commodity to police. There had been a slew of complaints against him, both in Chicago and the suburbs. 'Gacy is mentioned in several of the missing persons reports for these boys as someone the police interviewed, but not as a suspect,' Nelson said. 'Had they just gone a little bit further, they might have discovered what was going on.'

The victims, Nelson said, were very vulnerable. 'From a sociological standpoint, Gacy was preying on some of these kids who were not as well off. These were kids down on their luck, looking for money or a job, looking to better themselves, and here comes this businessman who's going to help them out … I was also surprised to learn how many of the victims knew and interacted with each other.'

By the end of 1977, John Wayne Gacy had raped, tortured and murdered twenty-eight young men and boys. As the year faded to black, Gacy must have felt omnipotent. The last act was coming, but Gacy didn't know it.

13

1978 – Beginning of the End

On New Year's Eve 1977 – a year and ten days before John Wayne Gacy admitted to everything – an eighteen-year-old North Side youth had a story to tell the cops. A local businessman named John Wayne Gacy had kidnapped him at gunpoint from a bus stop, said Robert Donnelly, and then forced him into performing sexual acts against his will. The teen had been busted three months earlier when police nabbed him with a grand total of three joints. The police weren't interested in pursuing charges against the avuncular contractor.

'I was shocked,' Donnelly told the *Chicago Tribune* in January 1979. 'They [cops] would only say there was insufficient evidence. Both the cops and an assistant state attorney said that he [Gacy] was a solid citizen. I was practically pleading with them. I even told them that he bragged to me he had killed people and was going to kill me, but my pleas didn't do any good … They treated me like I was some kid who was stoned.'

Donnelly had been tortured, raped and dragged into the bathroom at Gacy's home where Gacy repeatedly dunked his head under water in the bathtub until he passed out. The encounter featured the full expression of Gacy's deep-rooted sadism. His captor tormented Donnelly with jibes like: 'Aren't we playing fun games tonight?' Eventually, the boy was in such agonising pain, he begged Gacy to kill him. Gacy snarled: 'I'm getting round to it.' But he didn't kill him.

Bizarrely, like the other unnamed victim in January 1978, Gacy let the kid go and drove him to his workplace, but there was a malevolent warning: if he complained to the police, they would almost certainly not believe him. And Gacy was right.

When Gacy was questioned, he admitted, that, yeah, he and the kid had engaged in the sexual acts described by the teen, some of them violent and sadistic. But the boy was a willing participant, the contractor told detectives.

According to documents seen by the *Tribune*, the decision not to prosecute Gacy was made by assistant state attorney Jerry Latherow. The lawyer said he was under a gag order and could not discuss the matter. The police report should have raised red flags. It didn't. Police later denied that the teen had told them Gacy had admitted to murdering people – or threatening to kill him. And law enforcement also denied that anyone had ever described Gacy as a 'solid citizen'.

Then came the excuses. 'It was a one-on-one situation with Gacy's word against the kid's,' one law enforcement source said. 'There were no witnesses. Gacy wanted us to believe that the kid turned him in because he [Gacy] wouldn't pay blackmail, and that sort of thing does happen.' Once more, Gacy had skated away from trouble. But from 9 December 1977, when he killed David Talsma, to 16 February 1978, Gacy abstained from murder. Maybe the close calls had unnerved him – for a while.

The year was 1978 and the Dallas Cowboys bested the Denver Broncos in Super Bowl XII. The Great Blizzard of 1978 hammered Chicago, the Great Lakes and the Ohio Valley, leaving dozens dead; and punk-rock pioneers the Sex Pistols performed their final concert at Winterland Ballroom in San Francisco.

This is the year that would see Gacy reach the apex of his political involvement when a photo was snapped of the rotund businessman with First Lady Rosalynn Carter on 6 May. He had been the director of Chicago's annual Polish Constitution Day Parade since 1975 and would supervise the bash until the fateful year of 1978. It was through the parade and his political involvement that he would meet – and be photographed with – the First Lady at a private reception. On 21 January 1979 after Gacy's arrest, the *Chicago Sun-Times* published the photo revealing Carter's autograph: 'To John Gacy, Best Wishes – Rosalynn Carter'. It was a huge embarrassment to the U. S. Secret Service. Visible in the photo is an 'S' pin on the serial killer's lapel. It indicated he had been given special clearance.

That year was also a busy one for other serial killers. Boy-next-door monster Ted Bundy – who later confessed to murdering thirty women – went on a rampage at the Chi Omega Sorority House at Florida State University in Tallahassee having escaped police custody for a second time. On 15 January 1978, Bundy slipped into the sorority where he bludgeoned Margaret Bowman, twenty-one, with a piece of oak firewood as she slept, then garrotted her with a nylon stocking. Next, Bundy attacked twenty-year-old Lisa Levy. The maniac beat her unconscious, strangled her, tore off one of her nipples, bit deeply into her left buttock and sexually assaulted her with a hair mist bottle. Three other women were also attacked, suffering serious injuries. Detectives later determined that the attack took less than fifteen minutes and, remarkably, more than thirty possible witnesses heard not a peep. But Bundy had left something behind: a semen sample.

Now, the killer was running hard, but not hard enough to quench his bloodlust. In Lake City, Florida, he murdered twelve-year-old Kimberly Dianne Leach, who disappeared from school and whose remains were found seven weeks later. She had been raped and stabbed in the neck. As Bundy raced across the Florida Panhandle in a stolen car, he was pulled over in a Volkswagen Beetle, his favoured car to steal, by a cop in Pensacola. After a struggle, he was arrested.

He mumbled in the police cruiser: 'I wish you had killed me.'

* * * *

In Sacramento, California on 28 January, Richard Chase – the Vampire of Sacramento – was also arrested. A cannibal and necrophile, Chase ticked all the boxes that make a first-class psycho. After a lifetime of general weirdness, Chase began killing on 29 December 1977, when he shot to death a father of two in a drive-by.

The second victim was a three-months-pregnant young woman named Teresa Wallin, who was also shot to death on 23 January 1978. This time, Chase had sexual intercourse with her corpse as he stabbed her with a butcher's knife. And in a macabre twist, he removed her organs, cut off a nipple and drank her blood. As a final indignity, he stuffed dog feces down her throat.

Four days later he broke into the home of thirty-eight-year-old Evelyn Miroth and her boyfriend Danny Meredith. He proceed to murder Meredith with the Saturday Night Special .22-calibre handgun he carried. Miroth, her six-year-old son Jason, and her twenty-two-month-old nephew David Ferreira were next. Chase then mutilated Miroth and had sex with her corpse before cannibalising her. He then fled in Meredith's car and took little David Ferreira's body with him after being interrupted by a knock on the door. An alarmed neighbour had called cops.

Chase's handprints were all over the place. When police arrested him they found his apartment was soaked in blood. For his troubles, he was sentenced to die in the gas chamber at San Quentin. He knocked himself off on death row before the executioner could do the deed.

* * * *

Serial killer news from elsewhere aside, Gacy's evil compulsions were merely muted. Gacy would kill again soon.

The next victim would be the last he would bury in the crawl space. William Kindred, nineteen, was called Billy by his family and friends. Like many of Gacy's victims, he too hailed from rough-and-tumble Uptown, which had proved such a fertile hunting ground for the killer over the years. But how a street-smart kid like Billy Kindred ended up in Gacy's clutches remains something of a mystery. Billy was older, wiser and he wasn't a hustler. Nearly every night, Billy Kindred would visit his girlfriend, Mary Jo Paulus. And then, two days after Valentine's Day in 1978, he failed to show up.

Cops later 'developed information' that indicated that, on the night of 16 February 1978, Kindred had been picked up by his killer near Diversey and Broadway on the North Side. But no one does an intentional vanishing act by leaving their clothes and belongings behind, as Billy did in his New Town apartment.

For Paulus, it was the start of a lonely, desperate and ultimately tragic search. Most nights after work from her job as an office clerk, she would drive and walk around Chicago searching for Billy. She turned over every stone in the neighbourhood, then went beyond to encompass the entire metropolis in her search. The heartbroken young woman told the *Tribune* she had vowed to herself not to stop searching until Billy was found.

'It just wasn't normal for somebody who loves you – and who you love – to just disappear into thin air,' Paulus, then eighteen, told reporters as she wiped away tears. 'Deep down inside I figured something was very, very, very wrong. I just couldn't believe that he just up and left me without a word.'

Theirs was a story of young love. The couple had met in July 1977 – when Billy had picked up Mary Jo and a girlfriend while they were hitch-hiking on the city's North Side – and had been inseparable ever since. 'He was such a wonderful guy,' she sobbed. 'We were in love, and we talked about getting married as soon as he found a decent job.'

What she didn't and couldn't have known was that Billy had fallen into the clutches of John Wayne Gacy. Ten months later, when the news broke about the house of horrors on Summerdale Avenue, she became frightened that maybe Billy might be among the dead buried beneath the house.

'I cried and cried and couldn't stop,' she said of her reaction to the news. 'It was like instinct. I figured Billy's got to be under the house, too. Billy was young, handsome, muscular, and did odd jobs around the city – just like most of those victims. I even called Billy's sister and even told my mother that I felt Billy was under that house.'

A little over a month after Kindred's disappearance, Gacy had the itch again. Whether it was for murder or violent sex, it was much the same to him.

On 21 March 1978, Gacy was cruising in his Oldsmobile when he spotted Jeffrey Rignall. The attack on Rignall would turn into another missed opportunity for police to save lives and capture a killer. They didn't even have to do anything; Rignall would do all the heavy work for them. The lesser charge of battery would not even have been made against Gacy if it hadn't been for Rignall's determination to find his attacker. Nine months after Rignall went to cops, the lid blew off the Gacy case.

Rignall's life was forever haunted by his monstrous encounter with Gacy. Interestingly, in later accounts, Rignall claimed there was another man in the room as Gacy delighted in his torture and defilement. He would be called as a defence witness at Gacy's trial in their bid to prove the accused was insane. At one point during the trial, he vomited as he recounted his ordeal. He later wrote a book with Wilder entitled *29 Below* about his quest to find the identity of the man who raped and tortured him. Today, the book is out of print and copies can go for hundreds of dollars. He died at the young age of forty-nine in 2001 with Wilder at his side.

The close calls appeared to be getting to Gacy. His killing had tapered off dramatically. There were no more 'doubles'. Still, he carried on as usual. Another reason Gacy may have curtailed his sinister activities is that his crawl space was now crammed with bodies, meaning there was no room for new victims. It was at this point that Gacy decided he would toss new victims off a bridge and into the Des Plaines River.

After he murdered Billy Kindred on 16 February 1978, Gacy did not strike again until some time in mid-June of that year. The victim was Timothy O'Rourke. Gacy then again went dormant. He was arrested and charged in July with battery on Rignall and perhaps he was keeping his nose clean. He would wait nearly five months before he killed again. On 4 November 1978, he took the life of Frank Landingin. Then, shortly after his last Thanksgiving, James Mazzara met Gacy and was never seen again.

For John Wayne Gacy, now thirty-six years old, the coming weeks were about to change everything. After years of getting away with some of the most horrific crimes in American history, he was poised to make a mistake that would send him to death row.

During the previous six years, many of Gacy's victims had been the sorts of kids who might be written off as runaways.

148

His run of terror was blessed by both police indifference and the culture of the seventies. Many of the young men were poor, transient and from rough inner-city neighbourhoods – particularly the 'Hillbilly Heaven' of Uptown. Gacy also presented a largely respectable figure – despite all the gossip about his sexual preferences. Gacy could trust that the cops would believe him, rather than any victim who survived an encounter with him.

Robert Piest, though, would be a completely different kettle of fish. And Robert would be the final victim of the man who would soon publicly be known as 'The Killer Clown'.

14

Smartest Guy in the Room

There had been some close calls for John Wayne Gacy in 1978, but the now accomplished killer believed he was the smartest guy in the room. Time after time, he had slipped through the clutches of the police. Family, friends and neighbours didn't suspect a thing. And Gacy maintained his faith in his own cleverness until the minute they jabbed a needle in his arm sixteen years later.

Not only had Gacy been adept at escaping the attention of cops, neighbours and petrified parents, but he had made measured choices when it came to his victims. Most were runaways and hustlers from Chicago's rougher neighbourhoods, where parental attention and care were often in short supply. They were young men who would go under the radar. But some of his victims were from good families in the suburbs and they had continued to demand answers about the fate of their missing boys. They were not content to listen to law-enforcement bromides. Still, despite this, no real connection had been made to Gacy. And then Gacy made a mistake. No fast-talking bullshit would get him off the hook this time – although that didn't mean he wouldn't try.

The airwaves that Christmas season in 1978 featured the syrupy sweet 'You Don't Bring Me Flowers' by Barbra Streisand and Neil Diamond and disco smash 'Le Freak' by Chic. On 11 December, gangsters associated with the Lucchese crime family in New York City stole $6 million in cash and jewellery from Lufthansa. The heist was later immortalised on the big screen in Martin Scorsese's iconic mob movie *GoodFellas*.

Across the country in Chicago, another big crime story was unfolding, even if the participants were oblivious to the events about to unfold. It was 11 December 1978 – almost two years to the day that Greg Godzik had vanished. John Wayne Gacy had scored a lucrative contract to remodel suburban pharmacies and was making his rounds that afternoon. One of his stops was the Nisson Pharmacy in Des Plaines. He was there to discuss remodelling the store with owner, Phil Torf.

A fifteen-year-old stock boy named Robert Piest, who worked part-time at the store earning extra cash, overheard the conversation. What caused Piest's ears to prick up was Gacy mentioning that his company often hired teen boys. He would start them at $5 an hour, nearly double what Piest was pulling down at the pharmacy. What Piest didn't know, and could not have known, was that Gacy was also looking for something a little extra.

On that bitterly cold night, the honour student at Maine West High School was scheduled to celebrate his mother's birthday and she came to collect the star athlete in the car. 'Mom, wait a minute. I've got to talk to a contractor about a summer job that will pay me $5 an hour,' Piest told his mother, asking her to wait inside the store.

Piest was going to talk inside the contractor's Oldsmobile and get more details. His father Harold Piest later told reporters, 'That's the last anybody saw of him. It was his mother's birthday and we were waiting at home with cake.' The disappearance was utterly random and completely out of character for their son. 'He had never met him [Gacy] before. He approached Rob that night about this "summer job",' Harold Piest said. His son had wanted to buy a car. When Robert didn't return to the pharmacy, his mother Elizabeth drove home and called the police.

Piest had been taken to Gacy's house to hash out the summer job deal. The garrulous killer later told detectives that he had asked the handsome young man if there was 'anything he wouldn't do for the right price'. Robert Piest said he was only interested in working hard. Gacy doubled down, suggesting that the teenager could make 'good money' from hustling. Piest was dismissive of Gacy's suggestion. That's when the maniac tricked Piest with the 'handcuff trick'.

And after Piest was manacled, Gacy told him, 'I'm going to rape you, and you can't do anything about it.' With those chilling words, Gacy said his victim began sobbing, and he then placed a rope around his neck and strangled him to death. As Piest lay dying, Gacy left the room to take a phone call.

What Gacy didn't realise was that he had picked the wrong kid. Robert Piest was not a boy from Uptown, hustling for his money. He was a star athlete and an honour student. He was responsible. And so his family was justifiably alarmed when he failed to return to the drug store as promised. They filed a missing person report.

Pharmacy owner Phil Torf said that the contractor Piest had probably left the store with would have been local businessman, John Wayne Gacy. This time, the cops were interested. Very much so. The report came across the desk of Des Plaines Police Lieutenant Joseph Kozenczak. Coincidentally, his son also attended Maine West High School, where the missing Robert Piest was a popular student. To his eternal credit, Kozenczak, after speaking with the missing boy's mother, quickly determined the kid was not a runaway. And he decided that this Mr. Gacy warranted a closer look.

'We tried to get some direction on where to go with this thing,' Kozenczak recalled. 'We decided that since Gacy was the only name we had, maybe we could do a background check on the guy.' Detective Jim Pickell was charged with doing that.

The result, Kozenczak later said, was like 'throwing gasoline on a fire'. As Kozenczak told the tale, Pickell came running in and said: 'This guy was in the pen in Iowa for sodomy.' And Chicago cops had Gacy in the system, too, for alleged batteries on young men – all with sexual overtones. 'The real Gacy case just started right there,' he said.

On 12 December 1978, Kozenczak and two detectives visited Gacy at his home on Summerdale Avenue the next night. 'In my mind, I assumed Gacy had this kid prisoner and was abusing him. I didn't really think the kid was dead. I thought he would be battered and we'd have to prove the case against this guy Gacy ... There was a feeling I'd never had before on the job, a feeling that this kid was probably hurt real bad ... I don't know if it was the atmosphere: two squads going to see this guy; it was night; it was cold; a movie routine ... I said, "I'll betcha he's got this kid tied up, a prisoner in this house," and [Detective Jim] Pickell said, "Yeah, maybe." ... We parked in front of the house, Pickell and I went to the front. I sent Olson and Sommerschield around to the side. It was an access point to his garage. I just wanted them to keep an eye on the back part of the house ... We started knocking on the front door. In front of the house, there was this old street lamp. The globe threw light in the window of the front door ... The house was dark, but I saw somebody through this diamond-shaped window in the door, standing a foot and a half back, just staring. I said to Pickell, "There's somebody in there looking at us." Then he disappeared.'

Unsurprisingly, they soon had a guest. 'A van drove up and a kid jumped out and said, "Hey, you looking for John?" Just like nothing was going on. Now, if I saw four guys standing around in topcoats and suits, I'd think, "These guys are the cops," and maybe that's because I've been around it so long.'

The kid informed the detectives: 'You won't get him. He never answers the front door. You gotta go around back, to the family room.'

The detectives then went around to the back of the bungalow. Kozenczak looked through the window. 'There was John Gacy, sitting in an easy chair, drinking Pepsi and watching TV.' They knocked on the back door.

'I couldn't answer the door because I was in the john,' the blustering clown told the detectives. While Gacy was wily, Kozenczak was smarter. He decided to tell the killer a lie: that, yeah, he *had* been spotted talking to Robert Piest. 'He [Gacy] just stayed mute, didn't deny it or affirm,' the detective recalled. 'To me, that meant a lot. He just kind of stared for a while. Then he said: "I might have talked to one of the boys about some shelves that were thrown out in back. I don't remember who it was."' Gacy was evasive. He claimed he returned to the pharmacy because he had accidentally left his appointment book at the job site. Yeah, he'd seen two teens working at the pharmacy and yeah, he had asked one whether there were any building materials stashed behind the store. Maybe it was this Robert Piest. He wasn't sure. But no, he hadn't offered the kid a job.

Kozenczak pressed on: 'The parents are very concerned about their missing son, and seeing as you were the last one to see him, I'd like you to come down to the station and give us a statement.' He agreed to come by the cop shop for questioning but maybe after eight p.m. – as his uncle had just died. If he was rattled, Gacy quickly returned to form when the police pressed him. 'You guys are very rude. Don't you have any respect for the dead?' Gacy snarled. 'I know this kid is missing. But that's not important to me.'

The cop replied, getting angrier by the second: 'Well, it's important to the parents.' They were done. Gacy promised he would come by the station.

On the way down the driveway, Kozenczak told two of his detectives to drive up the block and keep an eye on Gacy and stick to him like glue. But within two minutes, they reported they had lost Gacy. Gacy had had his young employee, Mike Rossi, back up the P. D. M. van while the suspicious contractor got in his own car and drove away.

He was 'driving like a maniac' and the two surveillance detectives could not keep up without killing someone. What the investigators could not have known was that Gacy had gone into his attic where the body of Robert Piest had been stashed. He had placed the body in the trunk of his car and drove on I-55 to the Des Plaines River, south of Joliet and dumped the boy's body into the frigid water.

At the station, the designated hour of 8 p.m. came and went and there was no Gacy. Instead, he rolled in around 3.20 a.m. He was covered in mud. He had been in a car accident he told the cops on duty.

Later that day, the thirty-six-year-old contractor was back at the police station and sitting in an interrogation room. Investigators asked Gacy to provide a written statement of his comings and goings on 11 December, the day Piest vanished. He doubled down on his original story that he had not offered Piest a job. As for the teenager's disappearance, he knew nothing about that. And his appointment book? Gacy claimed that Torf had called him about it. Torf denied this.

Police were still hoping against hope that Robert Piest was alive and that maybe Gacy was holding him prisoner. Gacy was put under surveillance around the clock. 'At the time when we first started the surveillance, we certainly were hoping to find Rob Piest alive, but that kind of evaporated rather quickly because, as the other people involved in the investigation were looking into Gacy's background and Gacy's name, they came up with it being mentioned in other reports of missing teenage young men,' retired Detective Mike Albrecht told *Esquire* in 2021. 'It became apparent that he was involved with other missing persons who have never been found. So, we knew we were probably dealing with more than one victim here. Certainly I didn't have any idea it would be thirty-three.'

On 13 December 1978, detectives got their search warrant for Gacy's home. Investigators discovered a treasure trove of eyebrow-raising items: police badges, a 6-mm Brevettata starter pistol and a syringe and hypodermic needle were found inside a cabinet in Gacy's bathroom. In addition, cops also discovered handcuffs and books on homosexuality and pederasty – with titles like *The Great White Swallow* and *Pretty Boys Must Die*. There were porn movies, capsules of amyl nitrate and an 18-inch dildo in his bedroom. There was also a two-by-four with two holes drilled into each end, bottles of Valium and atropine, and several drivers' licences were found in the north-west bedroom. They discovered a blue parka in the laundry room and underwear that was obviously too small for the rotund Gacy. There was the Maine West High School class-of-1975 ring bearing the initials J. A. S. And, notably, a Nisson Pharmacy photo receipt that had been tossed in the trash along with a length of nylon rope. Investigators also confiscated Gacy's black Oldsmobile and other vehicles connected to his contracting work. And then, they watched him.

At the same time, Gacy employee Michael Rossi dropped a dime on his boss and told investigators a P. D. M. employee named Gregory Godzik had disappeared in 1977, and another named Charles Hattula had been found drowned in an Illinois river earlier in 1978. One investigator made a phone call to Carole Hoff, the second Mrs. Gacy. She told them about the disappearance of John Butkovich, yet another former Gacy employee, who had vanished in 1975, following a dispute with Gacy over money. And that Maine West High School ring with the initials of J. A. S.? Detectives traced the ring to John Alan Szyc who had disappeared on 20 January 1977. His mother said the ring and a number of other items – including a television set – were missing from her son's apartment. By 15 December, detectives had learned of Jeffrey Rignall's horrific ordeal at the hands of Gacy and the pending battery charge connected to the assault.

The pieces of an insidious puzzle were beginning to come together. It would be Gacy's very large ego that would drive the final nails into his own coffin. In his mind, since his bluster and effusive personality had allowed him to wriggle out of trouble so far, he would charm the cops to the point where they'd say: 'Nah, can't be this guy.' Detective Mike Albrecht had been charged with keeping Gacy talking as they secured the search warrant for his property. He found Gacy affable. 'So, I had to small talk with Gacy for a while. I brought him into the back office and just sat down and talked with him to keep him busy for a while,' Albrecht said. 'I got along with Gacy. We talked and we got along. I mean, the guy was full of crap. He was a real bragger, he liked talking about himself. Told us how much money he had and all his property he owned in Nevada, Wisconsin, Minnesota and Florida. He was always talking about himself and I just let him go on a little bit because we had to build a relationship with him.'

The contractor had been under surveillance for three days. 'The surveillance was not covert. He knew who we were and why we were watching him. He would ask us why we were doing it,' Albrecht said. With his propensity for head games, Gacy taunted the detectives following him at every turn. He'd lead them on car chases – blowing through red lights and racing through the streets. Gacy even started inviting the detectives tailing him into restaurants for dinner, drinks in local watering holes and even into his own home.

'I made a decision early on when we were watching him that when Gacy would go into a public place, a cab, or into a bar or restaurant or store or something like that, we would follow him and go in with him. And if he went into a private residence, of course, then we wouldn't. We'd wait for him outside. From midnight to noon was when we watched him, and during that time period, a lot of times Gacy would drive around the city doing his job estimates. And then after that, we would end up stopping in some 24-hour restaurant and sitting and talking to him.'

On one occasion, Gacy invited Detective Mike Albrecht and his partner, who were tailing him, into a restaurant for a meal. Gacy talked about the subject nearest and dearest to his cold heart – himself. He mentioned his side gig as a clown and told the stunned detectives: 'You know ... clowns can get away with murder.'

But Gacy stayed on message: he didn't know Robert Piest, had nothing to do with his disappearance, and suggested that maybe, just maybe, the cops were busting his balls as a result of his numerous political connections. Or maybe it was his recreational drug use. Either way, he was an honest businessman who was in the clear. Gacy even told his curious neighbours that the 'cops were trying to pin a murder on me.' Then he would laugh. The clock was ticking, though; it was nearly time up for Gacy.

On 17 December, investigators questioned Mike Rossi. They wanted to know about John Szyc. Rossi told the sceptical cops that Gacy had sold him the Plymouth Satellite because Szyc needed money to move to California. A forensics team began examining the contractor's beloved black Oldsmobile. As they combed the car and then the trunk, they made a discovery. A cluster of what they suspected was human hair. The forensics team brought in dogs trained in searching for missing people to see if they smelled anything in the Oldsmobile. Piest's family had given cops a piece of clothing so the dogs could get his scent. One of the clever canines laid on the passenger seat of the car. The dog's handler told detectives that what they were seeing was a 'death reaction'. Piest's body had been in Gacy's vehicle.

The investigation was moving at a lightning pace. It was now all hands on deck for the Des Plaines Police Department with assistance from Chicago cops and the Cook County Sheriff's Department. They were going at Gacy around the clock.

It was now a week since Robert Piest had disappeared and the strain was beginning to show on Gacy. He didn't shave, appeared tired and anxious and was hitting the bottle hard. But his good-guy act wasn't working with the cops and the constant surveillance was unnerving him. So he decided to go on the offensive and launched a $750,000 civil suit against the Des Plaines Police Department, demanding they end their surveillance of him. That hearing was slated for 22 December.

Still, unbeknownst to Gacy, the case against him was building. That afternoon, the serial number on the photo receipt found in Gacy's kitchen trash bin was traced to Nisson Pharmacy clerk, seventeen-year-old Kimberly Byers, who worked with Piest. She told detectives she had worn Piest's parka on 11 December to keep away the cold blowing into the store. And she had put the photo receipt in the pocket before handing it back to him as he left the pharmacy for his meeting with a local contractor about a job. Gacy had lied. He previously told cops he had not spoken to or interacted with Piest on the fateful night of 11 December. And somehow the dead boy's coat had ended up in his laundry room.

Investigators were also still speaking to Rossi who told them that, in the summer of 1977, his boss had told him to spread ten bags of lime in the crawl space beneath his house. Rossi told them about being instructed to dig trenches in the crawl space – and said that he had strict instructions about where to dig and where not to. Kozenczak asked Rossi point blank: 'Where do you think Gacy stashed Robert Piest's body?' Rossi replied, 'Probably the crawl space.' But Rossi denied any involvement in the boy's disappearance or firm knowledge of his whereabouts. And then he lawyered up and refused to further co-operate. Kozenczak would later note that when asked about Piest's disappearance during a polygraph test, Rossi's answers were 'erratic and inconsistent'. The veteran detective could not come to a 'definitive' conclusion on whether the twenty-year-old was telling the truth about his knowledge of or involvement in Gacy's crimes.

Another Gacy employee, David Cram told investigators Gacy had tried to rape him in 1976. He was with Gacy when they returned to the home on Summerdale and Gacy allegedly turned white as a sheet when he noticed mud on his carpet. Cram said Gacy snatched a flashlight and went into the crawl space looking for any signs of disturbance in his private burial ground. Yes, Cram told the cops, he had been in the crawl space himself to spread lime and dig trenches. His boss had said were for drainage pipes. The trenches were two feet wide by six feet long and two feet deep.

One evening, Gacy once again invited the detectives charged with watching him, inside his house. One cop kept the talkative Gacy in conversation while his partner, Bob Schultz, excused himself to go to the bathroom. He was looking to write down the serial number on Gacy's Motorola TV that they believed may have belonged to John Szyc.

The last time the cops were inside, the house had been cold. As the cop flushed the toilet, the furnace in Gacy's house kicked in. Suddenly, the stench emanating from the heating ducts was unmistakable. It was the putrid smell of the rotting corpses beneath their quarry's home. Albrecht recalled: 'That odour from the heat, from the crawl space ... Bob said right away, "It smelled like a morgue."'

On the night of 20 December 1978, five days before Christmas, Gacy got in his car and ended up at the office of his lawyer, Sam Amirante. Albrecht and his partner Dave Hachmeister sat in their car outside the lawyer's office and waited. They suspected Gacy was meeting Amirante about his civil suit against the cops. They were wrong.

Amirante later recalled that Gacy looked like a mess. He was unshaven, dishevelled and wanted a drink – the hard stuff, preferably. His lawyer grabbed a bottle of whiskey from his car and poured them both a drink.

The young lawyer then asked his client what he wanted to discuss. Gacy picked up a copy of the *Chicago Daily Herald* – a newspaper that served the city's suburbs – and pointed to a page-one story on the disappearance of Robert Piest. Gacy then told his shocked lawyer: 'This boy is dead. He's dead. He's in a river.'

And then Gacy unburdened his troubled soul and told a mortified Amirante everything. He had 'been the judge ... jury and executioner of many, many people' Gacy told him. And had buried the majority of his victims beneath the crawl space of his suburban home. Five boys had been dumped into the Des Plaines River. The dead were 'hustlers', 'male prostitutes' and 'liars'. Unencumbered by shame, Gacy boasted about his 'rope trick'. Sometimes, he told Amirante, he would get up in the morning and find 'dead, strangled kids' in his home, their hands cuffed behind their backs. There were two reasons he had buried his victims in the crawl space, he told his lawyer: convenience, and he believed they were his property. The confession went on for hours and into the next morning.

As Amirante later told the tale, Gacy was putting a pretty big dent in the bottle of whiskey his lawyer had produced and eventually passed out halfway through the confession. While the killer slept, his lawyer made arrangements for a psychiatric appointment the next morning. No doubt he knew that an insanity defence would be the only card that could save his client from a date with the electric chair.

After sleeping it off for several hours, Gacy awoke in his lawyer's office and was told by Amirante he had spent the previous evening confessing to the slayings of around thirty men and boys and that he should see a psychiatrist.

'Well, I can't think about this right now. I've got things to do,' Gacy informed his lawyer, adding that he planned to skip the appointment with the psychiatrist because he had business to take care of.

Due to client attourney privilege, Amirante couldn't legally reveal what his client had told him to the cops sitting outside his office. But he had to do something. He flew outside and offered the detectives some spine-tingling advice. He said 'Don't let Gacy leave.' Albrecht recalled, 'He said block his car in. If he tries to leave, shoot his tires out!' But the detectives were still building a case against Gacy. One false step could jeopardise the entire investigation.

On his last day of freedom, Gacy later confessed that things were 'hazy'. He had come to terms with the fact that his arrest was inevitable and he spent the day saying his goodbyes to friends and clients. After leaving Amirante's office, the serial killer drove to a gas station where he filled up his rental car and gave the gas jockey a bag of reefer, which the kid turned over to cops. He eerily told the young man: 'The end is coming (for me). These guys are going to kill me.'

Next, he drove to his pal, fellow contractor Ronald Rhode's home. Gacy hugged his shocked friend and began sobbing. Gacy told Rhode: 'I've been a bad boy. I killed thirty people, give or take a few.'

The two detectives following him noticed he was holding a rosary to his chin, praying as he hit the expressway. His next stop was a meeting with his employees, Cram and Rossi, where he again confessed his sordid sins, which they later reported to cops.

Finally, Gacy had Cram drive him to a place of great symbolism and perhaps the root of his deadly rampage. The place was Maryhill Cemetery, the final resting place of his father and his tormentor, John Stanley Gacy, who had died in 1969. As Gacy knelt, sobbing, at his brutal father's grave, cops were outlining the draft of their second search warrant. The object was to find the body of the missing Robert Piest, whom they believed was buried in the crawl space.

But there were fears at this point regarding Gacy's increasingly erratic behaviour. Police worried he might be planning to kill himself. Cops did not want that so they decided to charge him with possession and distribution of the marijuana he had given the gas jockey.

While it may have appeared that the John Wayne Gacy Show was coming to an end, it wasn't. In fact, it was just beginning.

15

Black Christmas

Around 4.30 p.m. on 21 December 1978, Cook County Judge Marvin J. Peters granted cops a second search warrant to go through the crawl space at Gacy's house in their search for the body of Robert Piest. Detectives gave Gacy the news, and suddenly he sang like a canary. Piest wasn't there, he told them but … he murdered another young man in self-defence in the early seventies. That kid was buried under his garage.

Cops were only beginning to suspect what they might have on their hands. 'In Des Plaines … we've had homicides … but we never had a real kind of abduction or kidnapping,' Lieutenant Joseph Kozenczak told the *Chicago Sun-Times*.

Shortly after Judge Peters gave detectives the green light, they arrived with forensic technicians at the home on Summerdale Avenue. When they arrived, investigators discovered that the contractor had unplugged his sump pump, flooding his insidious crawl space with water. Cops replaced the plug and then waited for water to drain from the crypt. The crawl space was twenty-eight feet by thirty-eight feet.

The first man down in the hole was forensics technician Daniel Gentry. Gentry went to the south-west corner of the cold, dank space and started digging. The horror show didn't take long to get underway because, within minutes, Gentry had uncovered rotting flesh and a human arm bone. He yelled to his waiting colleagues, 'You can charge Gacy with murder.' And then the shocked forensics tech added: 'I think this place is full of kids.'

A call was put in to the Cook County Medical Examiner Dr. Robert Stein. It was a cop and he sounded frantic. 'There's a body or something in the crawl space of a ranch house near Norridge,' the unidentified officer told Stein, who quickly proceeded to Summerdale Avenue. 'I opened the door and, my God, there was this odour of death,' Stein told the *Chicago Tribune*.

Gentry was soon joined by a police photographer who began digging in the north-east corner. He found a patella, the small bone in front of the knee joint. The pair then went to the south-east corner of the crawl space and found two lower-leg bones. The macabre discoveries were much too decomposed to be Robert Piest. Another crime-scene technician discovered a skull beside the previously unearthed body in the north-east corner. More bones. More body parts. More horror. The scale of the carnage was unspeakable. Even veteran cops had never seen anything like this charnel house of human depravity.

Outside the house on Summerdale, onlookers started to gather with curiosity because of the big police presence. Back at police headquarters, Gacy, to date charged only with possession and distribution of marijuana, waited. He was eventually told that investigators had found human remains in the crawl space of his home. He would now be facing murder charges. Gacy had known this was coming. He had known it was inevitable after spilling his guts to his lawyer, Sam Amirante. In the early morning hours of 22 December 1978 – around maybe two or three a.m. – the suspected killer told cops he wanted to finally 'clear the air'.

Gacy sat down at a table in the interrogation room with Detective Mike Albrecht. With him were his lawyers. He began to tell his nightmarish tale.

'We were in a small interview room for the confession. Seated next to me was Gacy's lawyer Sam Amirante, and standing behind him was the other attorney, Leroy Stevens,' Albrecht recalled in 2021. 'Right across from me was Gacy. Getting statements from him, I asked him to explain several things that happened, and he was leaning back in his chair, kind of comfortable. I was there for three or four of these, and he never once showed any remorse. He always blamed the kids. It was their fault. They came to him for money, for drugs, for sex, for whatever it may be. And he specifically said, they put the ropes around their own neck. They got what they deserved. He never had any remorse in any way.

'But this particular time I'm trying to get his statement, he's leaning back in his chair. It was very late, two or three o'clock in the morning, and he had his eyes closed and he was talking. And we were talking back and forth.'

Albrecht was about to get a foreshadowing of Gacy's blockbuster trial two years in the future. His legal team was forming the building blocks of an insanity defence involving at least four different personalities. John Wayne Gacy had already waived his Miranda rights. Smoking cigarettes like there was no tomorrow, Gacy told cops that there were actually four 'Johns'. There was John the contractor, John the clown and John the politician. The fourth personality went by the name of Jack Hanley. Jack was the monster who murdered those boys. Jack was evil. Jack was the monster terrorising Chicago. Occasionally, he'd tell shocked detectives: 'You'll have to ask Jack about that.'

But whilst Gacy warmed up to the direction his lawyer was guiding him in, he wasn't able to be consistent. 'Amirante started calling him, trying to get his attention and he'd say,

"Jack, well, what about this? Jack, what about that?" To try to start a conversation by addressing "Jack",' Albrecht recalled. 'And Gacy never responded. After probably five times of trying to do that, finally I said, "John, your attorney's trying to get your attention." And Amirante was sitting right next to me, and he immediately responded. Amirante gave me a look of … "why'd you do that?" Because his little plan didn't work. He [Gacy] didn't respond to "Jack", but he responded to my "John" immediately.'

The details which were emerging from Gacy's confession to police were appalling. Gacy copped to murdering around thirty young men and boys. He knew some of their names, others he did not. And he insisted they were all male prostitutes or runaways. Like many killers, Gacy liked to keep souvenirs of his victims and investigators had found them by the bucketload: wallets, rings, drivers' licences, clothes and other knick-knacks. He boasted that he had only dug five of the graves. The rest of the trenches were excavated by his flunkies – including the missing Gregory Godzik – so Gacy would always 'have graves available' for the next kill. Once the crawl space was filled to capacity, Gacy told police that he had planned in January 1979 to seal the crypt of his creation forever by filling it with concrete. It was one dastardly deed he would never accomplish.

He had other plans for the future as well. Gacy believed he and Carole Hoff would get back together, ditch Chicago for a smaller town and open a fried-chicken restaurant. As the killer talked and talked, detectives finally asked him about the reason Gacy was sitting in that small room clouded with cigarette smoke – Robert Piest, whose disappearance had kicked off the investigation.

He quickly admitted to having lured Piest to his house and strangling him to death on 11 December. The ghoulish Gacy admitted sleeping beside Piest's lifeless body before ditching the corpse into the Des Plaines River early on 13 December after the police had arrived to question him.

'He talked about what he did to these young men, especially about Rob Piest,' Albrecht said. 'He went into pretty good detail on what happened, from the handcuff trick to the rope trick, to starting to strangle them in such a way that it was slow while he would perform oral sex on the victims … Not to repeat myself, but there was no remorse at all. He blamed these kids and he told us what he did to them in a matter-of-fact conversation, just like we're having right now. It was just, "This is what I did today. I killed somebody." And it didn't bother him.'

Cops had a vested interest in finding young Piest quickly and asked if Gacy would show them where he had dumped the body. Accompanied by uniformed and plain-clothes detectives and his older sister, Gacy was taken to the I-55 bridge two days before Christmas to show where he tossed the boy's body into the river.

Their next stop was the house on Summerdale Ave. There, Gacy was instructed to mark the concrete garage floor with orange spray paint to show detectives where he had buried the young man whom Gacy claimed he had killed in self-defence. It was the final resting spot of former P. D. M. employee John Butkovich, who he had murdered on 31 July 1975. When the killer was escorted into his house, he was reportedly mortified at the amount of mud staining his carpets and floors from the shoes of desperate cops searching for answers.

Back at the police station, Gacy offered to draw a map for cops to make it easier to find his victims in the crawl space. The rough drawing was sketched on a phone-message sheet. This caused Albrecht to scoff again at the notion that Gacy was insane. He realised that he knew exactly what he was doing. The diagram he drew proved it. 'He buried twenty-six bodies in the crawl space. He knew exactly where they were. If you looked at the diagram that was made, and they did the overlay at the trial of where the bodies were found, and his drawing, those drawings were exact,' Albrecht said. 'Almost exactly to a T of where all these bodies were. When he was drawing, he started with the first one where he put a little rectangle or X and said that was the first one because the first one he had put concrete over it after he'd buried him. And then from then on, he just had trenches dug by the two young men that worked for him. And he would just put them into those trenches.'

'[Gacy's] giving all kinds of statements, saying there's a body here, a body there, a body in a lake or a lagoon, a body buried,' frustrated Cook County Sheriff Richard Elrod told reporters. Over the next week, twenty-six bodies were retrieved from Gacy's crawl space. Investigators found three more corpses elsewhere on Gacy's property. The work was time-consuming, tedious, and heartbreaking. The forensic team went to a local McDonald's restaurant and got French-fry baskets to help them sift through the dirt. Lieutenant Joseph Kozenczak told his team to help themselves to a case of beer in Gacy's fridge, a small reward for the nightmarish work. As the bodies came out, the remains were placed into body bags before being transported to the Cook County Morgue. Medical examiner Robert Stein oversaw the macabre task.

Each body was identified with a number. The first remains that came out were identified as Victim No. 1. The victim had been buried in the north-east area of the crawl space under the room that Gacy had once used as an office. But Stein could not determine a cause of death.

Between Gacy's confession and where the bodies were buried, officers began to see a picture emerging of the timeline of the murders. It was determined that Victim No. 5, buried three feet under the soil, was the first unfortunate inhabitant of the mass grave.

Cops temporarily called off the search so that investigating officers could spend some time with their families over Christmas and get a respite from the horror. But on Boxing Day, 26 December, they were back at uncovering four more bodies from the dirt. Victims No. 6 and No. 7 were buried in the same grave, leading detectives to believe that the two youths had been murdered at the same time – one of Gacy's famous 'doubles'. One was discovered in a fetal position with a cloth rag stuffed in its mouth.

The story was making headlines around the globe as more victims were found. 'The three we found were under just one small section of the floor,' a sheriff's investigator told the *Chicago Tribune*. 'We don't know what we'll find when we rip up the rest of it.' What they would find was a nightmare of cruelty on an unimaginable scale. 'This is one of the most horrendous [cases] I have ever had anything to do with,' Cook County State Attorney Bernard Carey told reporters.

Victim No. 8 was found with the tourniquet used to strangle him still knotted around his neck. Victim No. 9 was found beneath a layer of concrete and was found to have several stab wounds to the ribs and sternum, suggesting he was likely Gacy's first victim – before he changed his modus operandi. On 27 December, eight more bodies were discovered. Victim No. 10 was buried face upwards, parallel to the wall of the crawl space directly beneath the entrance to Gacy's home. Both Victim No. 11 and Victim No. 12 – found face downwards with a ligature around their necks – were buried beside each other in the centre of the crawl space, directly beneath the hallway.

Victim No. 13 was found beneath the spare bedroom. Victim No. 14 and No. 15 were recovered from a common grave diagonal to Victim No. 10. Victim No. 14 and No. 15 were found with their heads and upper torsos inside separate plastic bags. Victim No. 16 was found close to Victim No. 13 who was found with a cloth rag lodged deep in his throat, which would have caused death by suffocation. Victim No. 17 was also found with a ligature around his neck.

In late December, investigators also identified the body of the teenager who was pulled naked out of the Des Plaines River weeks before, as Frank Landingin. His driver's licence had been discovered in Gacy's home, connecting the contractor to the boy's murder. On 28 December, police found the body of James 'Mojo' Mazzara in the same river. The coroner said he had suffocated on his own underwear.

Besides dealing with the graveyard on Summerdale Avenue and the bodies in the river, investigators were pulling out all the stops on learning everything they could about the accused. That meant talking to former employees, friends and family of Gacy. One of those was twenty-six-year-old Art Peterson. In the fall of 1977, Peterson had gone to the house on Summerdale. He was looking for a job and had seen a poster seeking workers for a suburban contractor.

'He asked me if I wanted to come in and have a beer,' Peterson later told the *Chicago Sun-Times*. 'He went to the bar and came out and the first thing he said was that he was bisexual. Then he said, "You could have punched me in the nose when I said that, but you didn't. Maybe I could get you interested, too."' Gacy made his pitch to Peterson – telling him that bisexuality was very fashionable, trendy even. But Peterson wasn't buying the proposition and the two men argued. 'I said, "John, do you want me to announce this publicly, tell the neighbours you're bisexual?" And he said, "Oh, they already know."'

Finally, Gacy made his move and tried to molest the young psychology graduate. And when Peterson tried to make a break for it he says, 'Gacy got really upset. He said he had a gun. He said, "Do you know how easy it would be to get one of my guns and kill you – and how easy it would be to get rid of the body? As a matter of fact, I already have killed some people."'

After all this, Peterson still went to work for Gacy but it was only for about two weeks. On the sexual front, the contractor remained persistent, unwilling to hear the word no. At one point, Gacy offered him $300 to $400 to have sexual relations with him. And, as an added bonus, he'd pay Peterson $10 an hour to be his travelling companion on business trips. Peterson torpedoed that idea and quit shortly afterwards because Gacy wasn't paying him enough for his labour. And he creeped Peterson out.

Another young man, twenty-three-year-old Dominic Joczinski, worked for Gacy for two years and told the *Tribune* that the boss's sexual appetite was a joke among his workers. He had tried it on with virtually every single one of them. And there was the bragging. Gacy told his workers lewd tales of having sex with big wheels in business and politics. And his construction business offered Gacy a ready supply of young men.

'He made advances to me, too,' Joczinski said. 'But I just told him to leave me alone, and he didn't bother me any more. He put on such a good façade for all the neighbours and everything – like he was such a successful businessman and all.'

Both Peterson and Joczinski said that while they had put the kibosh on Gacy's sexual overtures towards them, he always seemed to have two or three sexual partners among his workers. And the chilling fate of others who fell into Gacy's clutches was not lost on Joczinski. 'I'm freaked out. I'm just glad this didn't happen to me,' he said.

At the house, more bodies kept emerging from the crawl space. Each with its own melancholy coda. Some were found gagged, with ligatures around their necks. Two socks were recovered from one victim's pelvic region, another had a cloth stuffed down his throat.

On 30 December 1978, police had their first name: Victim No. 2 was John Butkovich, eighteen. By New Year's Day they had more: Gregory Godzik, seventeen; John Szyc, nineteen; and Rick Johnston, also seventeen. After her son was identified, Godzik's devastated mother told the *Sun-Times*, 'Up until now, I felt that, gee, maybe he got away. Maybe it wasn't him.'

And the names kept coming, a roll-call of tears. Some of the bones were commingled together. The final victim recovered from the crawl space was found beneath the washroom and buried ten inches below the soil's surface. He too had a cloth shoved down his throat.

On 8 January 1979, John Wayne Gacy was indicted for the murders of seven young men along with aggravated kidnapping, deviate sexual assault and taking indecent liberties with a child. Cook County State Attorney Bernard Carey threw in another bombshell: the state would be seeking the death penalty. Stunned authorities in liberal Chicago wanted to see John Wayne Gacy die in the electric chair. Gacy pleaded not guilty two days later even as the evidence of his depravity unfolded.

The arrival of the Chicago Blizzard – a huge snowstorm – in 1979, which lasted from 13 January to 17 January meant that police suspended operations once again at the house. The snow and the unusually cold weather left the ground frozen, making excavation difficult for the next two months. The search resumed in March even as Gacy claimed that all the bodies had now been recovered. At this point, twenty-six sets of remains had been removed from the house … why would he lie?

However, on 9 March, Victim No. 28 was found wrapped within several plastic bags and buried beneath the patio around fifteen feet from the barbecue pit in Gacy's backyard. On 16 March – the day before Gacy's birthday – Victim No. 29 was found beneath the dining room floor.

It was grim, disturbing work. Stein, the medical examiner, said the victims recovered from the nondescript bungalow at 8213 W. Summerdale Avenue were all in an advanced state of decomposition. Using evidence provided by some of the victims' families, investigators continued to try to identify the unfortunate young men and boys. At least twenty-three of the victims were identified by means of dental records. Others were identified from X-rays of past broken bones and the trove of souvenirs Gacy had purloined from the dead.

But, in some cases, identification wasn't going as quickly as investigators had hoped. There were cases where dental records and X-rays didn't exist, but there was also something else. It was thought that some parents of the missing boys did not come forward because of the homosexual aspect of the insidious crimes. Police later reasoned, that because of the stigma attached to homosexuality at the time, they were too ashamed to come forward or even countenance that their sons may have been gay. 'I'm surprised we haven't had more calls from parents. Maybe they cannot imagine their sons getting involved in a case with homosexual overtones,' Sergeant Howard Anderson of the Cook County Sheriff's office told the *Chicago Tribune*.

Finally, on 19 April 1979, the body of the young man whose disappearance had been the start of the investigation was found in the Illinois River, a tributary of the Des Plaines River. It was the body of fifteen-year-old Robert Piest. The next day, the police investigation concluded at the now wrecked house at 8213 West Summerdale Avenue. And Cook County workers began completely demolishing the house of horrors.

One of the workers who had the ghoulish task of recovering the bodies from Gacy's home later noted the aura of evil that lurked in the bland bungalow. 'If the devil's alive, he lived here,' he sadly said.

16

Identifying the Dead

In 1979, the world was in a state of turmoil. The Shah of Iran had been booted from the Peacock Throne and a dour, unknown cleric named Ayatollah Khomeini would turn the country into a strict Islamic theocracy which would fight with Gacy for the headlines. On the same day, Khomeini flew into Tehran from his Paris exile, the Sex Pistols' notorious bass player Sid Vicious died of a heroin overdose. American football's Pittsburgh Steelers won the Super Bowl, sealing their claim as the 'Team of the Seventies'. On 3 May 1979, Margaret Thatcher was elected prime minister of the United Kingdom with a mandate for change. And back in Chicago, the grim work detectives had begun in December came to a close.

After Gacy's house had been ploughed under, leaving an empty lot, cops decided they should try to auction off some of the non-evidentiary items that had been retrieved. Among these items were clown heads, stereo equipment, furniture and tools that would go on the auctioneers' block at Kane County Fairgrounds.

Authorities hoped that the money raised would help pay for the accused killer's defence so it wouldn't all be on the public purse. However, Gacy's lawyer Sam Amirante asked that the auction be called off, partly because it was slated to happen on Father's Day. 'I'm not sure it's the proper way to get the money,' Amirante said at the time. In October, Cook County eventually agreed to foot the bill for Gacy's legal eagles. By this point Gacy's lawyers were more than $2,000 in debt trying to conjure up a strategy to defend the most hated man in America. 'If we ever make a profit on this case, we would be glad to reimburse the county,' Sam Amirante joked to reporters.

The knick-knacks, clown memorabilia and everything else would stay in storage for the next fifteen years. Gacy's prized 1979 Oldsmobile Delta 88 – used to carry at least one of the boy's bodies, Robert Piest's – was apparently sold at an auction in nearby Winnebago County near the Wisconsin border, north of Chicago in 1980. The auction also featured automobiles that had been owned by Muhammad Ali, Elvis Presley and former U. S. President Gerald Ford.

As 1979 rolled on, not a week went by without some new bit of chilling information emerging into the public sphere about the crimes commited by John Wayne Gacy. Gacy, now thirty-seven, had already been charged with the murders of seven youths. On 23 April 1979, a Cook County grand jury tagged him for an additional twenty-six murders to make a total of thirty-three – at the time it was the most ever attributed to a single killer in American history.

By the end of May 1979, seventeen of the victims had been identified: Billy Kindred, Greg Godzik, Frank Landingin, John Butkovich, John Szyc, Rick Johnston, James Mazzara, Michael Bonnin, Robert Gilroy, John Prestidge, Russell Nelson, Timothy O'Rourke, John Mowery, Matthew Bowman, Billy Carroll, Robert Piest and Randall Reffett had all been identified and their broken families notified.

Police were still trying to identify at least sixteen victims and turned to the public with items they had recovered from the house in the hope of putting names to bodies. There were jackets, shirts, jeans, a Boy Scout wristwatch, necklaces and belt buckles.

On 28 August that year, Judge Louis Garippo ruled that all the charges against Gacy would be heard at one trial. 'It is apparent that it would not serve the ends of justice to fragment the prosecution into thirty-three separate prosecutions,' Garippo said in his ruling. The trial date was slated for 7 January 1980. On 12 September 1979, two more of the bodies were identified. Young husband and father, Tommy Boling and Michigan runaway, Robert Winch who had disappeared within days of each other in 1977 and were discovered buried side by side in Gacy's crawl space. Cops confirmed that they had identified Winch by his distinctive tiger's-eye belt buckle and fracture markings on his bones.

November brought the identification of yet another victim. This time it was Samuel Stapleton, fourteen, whose remains were identified by a dental X-ray. He had vanished on 13 May 1976 while walking home from his sister's house. Cops had found the boy's bracelet on one of the bodies found in the crawl space. 'He was just like any other kid, he'd get picked up for curfew violation,' his mother Bessie told reporters. 'Fine. He was no runaway.' Sadly, his parents' worst fears had been realised.

Two days later, police also had an identification for David Talsma, with the help of an X-ray of a broken arm. He had been missing since 14 December 1977. The day he was identified would have been his twenty-first birthday and it brought the total of identified victims to twenty-one.

Gacy was a notorious liar and a bullshit artist par excellence and he continued to play the cops, even though he was now safely caged. The serial killer had lied when he told investigators they had found all the bodies in March of 1979. Investigators had found two more. And then more. He was always vague about how many he had killed. Already, many investigators and serial-killer experts suspected Gacy's savage quest for sex and death had extended beyond the Chicago area.

Detective Rafael Tovar recalled a chilling encounter with the killer in the days leading up to his trial. 'I was transferring him from our police lock-up to the county lock-up. Just in conversation, I asked him, "John. There are a lot of numbers going around. How many people did you kill?"' At this point Gacy told him he thought that forty-five sounded like 'a good number'. 'So I asked him, "Well, where are they?"' Tovar recalled. 'He said, "No. That's your job to find out." He was the type of guy that – if he knew that you knew something or that you were going to find out – he'd be totally honest with you. If he didn't think that you were going to find out, he liked to play mind games with you. I believe him. Everything else he told me was true, so I believe that there are more [victims] out there.'

During the investigation, Gacy was locked up in the Cook County Jail and kept in segregation because any con who jammed a knife into his guts would be a hero that even the most hard-assed cops might approve of.

Like the detectives investigating him, Amirante got to know Gacy very well. Before Gacy's confession to him and his subsequent arrest, they had known each other in passing, through local Democratic politics. Amirante had even spent time in Gacy's home discussing local politics over a beer. Amirante was thirty years old at the time and had been a member of the Cook County public defenders' office but, he later told the *Chicago Tribune*, was preparing to hang his own shingle and specialise in personal injury work – that lucrative area of law, much advertised on American airwaves. Then he got the fateful call that would change his life forever – the John Wayne Gacy horror show had unfolded. Standing just five foot two inches tall, Amirante later joked to the Chicago newspapers that before he took on Gacy as a client, he was six foot four inches. 'And this is all that's left of me,' he said.

Amirante recognised that the insanity defence was Gacy's only chance of not facing the death penalty. But Chicagoans wanted the contractor to fry. Amirante became a close number two to his client in the most-hated sweepstakes. In a 1994 interview, Amirante was philosophical about why he defended Gacy and about his client's personality. 'I dedicated fifteen months of my life to this man for nothing more than the love of the law and the fact that he asked me to represent him,' Amirante told the *Chicago Tribune* in 1994. 'I gave it my all, and I lost a lot of friends because of it. People hated me as much as him, if not more, because I was the guy trying to save him. I got all kinds of death threats. A lot of people hate me to this day, and I'm the kind of guy who likes to be liked. I'm very idealistic, and I lost a lot because of that case … It was tough on my family, tough on my wife, tough on our marriage. But like Rocky said, "A man's got to do what a man's got to do."'

In the year leading up to his trial, Gacy was on ice at the Menard Correctional Center in Chester, Illinois, around 355 miles south of Chicago, off the I-55 where, further north, the serial killer had dumped bodies into the Des Plaines River. The prison sat on a bluff overlooking the Mississippi River. In the run-up to the trial, Gacy spent more than 300 hours with psychiatrists, for both the defence and the prosecution, who put him through a battery of psychological tests. The results would be put in front of a panel of psychiatrists who would determine whether the bombastic Chicagoan was mentally competent to stand trial.

Gacy played along. Once again he feigned suffering from multiple personality disorder. Jack Hanley was back in the picture as the personality responsible for the murders. Jack was now a rotten cop. This was 'Bad Jack'. Gacy told psychiatrists that, when he had confessed his sinister crimes to detectives, he was relaying the crimes of 'Bad Jack'. 'Bad Jack', Gacy said, hated homosexuality and viewed male prostitutes as 'weak, stupid and degraded scum'. Gacy even convinced some of them and a few thought that maybe, just maybe, he suffered from multiple personality disorder. Others who examined him thought he could be a paranoid schizophrenic.

Gacy would plead not guilty by reason of insanity to the charges. His lawyers would take a page from the Robert Louis Stevenson novella, *The Strange Case of Dr. Jekyll and Mr. Hyde*. But even Sam Amirante seemed never to quite know what John Wayne Gacy would do next. He later told an anecdotal Gacy story that, to him, illustrated his client's personality. 'This sums it up: my dad had a big Lincoln Continental. It was his pride and joy,' Amirante told the *Tribune* in 1994. 'Someone wrote on it: "Your son must be gay. Only a queer would represent John Gacy." My dad made a police report and it made the papers. Gacy read about it and he called me at my house. My mom and dad were there. Gacy says he wants to apologise to my dad. I said, "Tell him yourself." And I give the phone to my dad. I said, "Dad, it's John Gacy." He gets real red, but he takes the phone and I hear him say, "Hi, thanks, bye." [Afterwards] I said "What did he say?" He said Gacy told him, "I'm really sorry about what happened to your car. You know there are a lot of nuts out there."'

Amirante was faced with another problem when it came to trial. Media coverage had been wall to wall, not just in the local area and the wider Midwest; the Gacy story had shocked and appalled the entire nation, along with the rest of the world. In Chicago, where Gacy committed all of his known murders, the jury pool – even in the nation's second biggest city – would be hopelessly tainted. So his legal team requested a change of venue, charging that 'there is a pattern of deep-rooted prejudice' against Gacy in Cook County due to 'pervasive' and 'emotionally packed' media coverage. Other legal experts suggested that a jury selected in Rockford would be likely to be more rural, more conservative and less likely to buy the insanity defence that Amirante was planning on. In more sophisticated and diverse Chicago, they felt that gambit had a better chance of working.

On 7 January 1980, Judge Joseph Garippo made a compromise. He ruled that the jury – twelve jurors and two alternates – would be selected in Rockford in Winnebago County, ninety minutes north-west of Chicago, near the Wisconsin border. 'I find that there is a substantial decrease in publicity outside Cook County,' Garippo said. 'Perhaps surprisingly so.' The prosecution did not object. 'We are not really adversaries,' William Kunkle told the court. 'We have no objection to getting a fair trial for the defendant.'

But, and it was a big but, the trial would stay in Chicago. Garippo reasoned that it would be easier on Cook County coffers to sequester the jurors in the Windy City than to put up prosecutors, defence lawyers, court personnel, witnesses and cops in hotels in Rockford. He expected the Gacy trial would be long and expensive. In the instance of Gacy versus Illinois, not everyone would be able to relocate to Cook County for a trial expected to last six weeks so officials in Winnebago County summoned more than 350 potential jurors. Normally, the county would summon 135 for a major trial. Fourteen people would be chosen: twelve regular jurors and two alternates in the event of sickness or some other emergency. These would be the people who would sit in judgement of John Wayne Gacy.

As the arrangements for the jury were made, the trial was delayed. On 26 January 1980, Gacy was moved to an isolated area on the third floor of the Winnebago County Jail next to the courthouse, prior to jury selection.

Facing off against Amirante would be William Kunkle, who was chief deputy in the state attorney's office. It would be his job to prove that Gacy was sane and deserved to die in the electric chair. The task for the thirty-seven-year-old prosecutor was equal to the one Amirante faced. During jury selection, more than half the jurors told Judge Garippo they believed that anyone who would torture, rape and murder thirty-three people, then bury them under their house 'had to be crazy'.

'Gacy's actions were clearly planned. One of the defence psychiatrists said he believed Gacy had brief psychotic episodes during the murders,' Kunkle later said. 'It's hard to dig trenches in advance of an anticipated, brief psychotic episode. Another defence psychiatrist said Gacy was amnesic and couldn't remember the details of the killings or the disposal of the bodies.' Kunkle and the prosecution had to disprove any notion, once and for all, that Gacy was not insane. He was evil. '[We were] much less interested in why somebody does something as opposed to did he have criminal intent? I absolutely agreed with the state's experts that Gacy is a criminal, he's evil, he's a liar, a conman, devious and self-serving,' Kunkle said.

Chicago, the nation and the world held their breath: John Wayne Gacy was about to be judged by a jury of his peers. What no one knew was that the Gacy story wouldn't end with his trial – it would have legs like a malevolent spirit, returning to haunt all and sundry for decades afterwards.

17

Judgement Days

On Wednesday 6 February 1980, the weather in Chicago was freezing, overcast and gloomy with a light dusting of snow. Just over two years since the disappearance of fifteen-year-old honour student Robert Piest, suburban contractor John Wayne Gacy was going on trial for the torture, rape and murder of thirty-three young men and boys.

A little more than a month away from his thirty-eighth birthday, the accused killer would now find himself in the fight of his life – *for* his life. In June 1977, the state of Illinois had reinstated the death penalty so any murder Gacy was proven to have committed after that date could be punishable by execution. Failure to secure a not-guilty by reason of insanity verdict would result in a one-way ticket to death row in Menard, southern Illinois and the electric chair.

All eyes were on Chicago, where the man – who if found guilty of what he was accused of would be the worst serial killer in American history – was slated to go on trial. The jury consisted of seven men and five women and the Cook County Criminal Court Building at 46th St. and California in Chicago would be the arena where Gacy's life would be saved or lost.

With the sheer weight of all the physical evidence, the confessions of the accused and an army of witnesses, it looked like it would be a slam dunk for the prosecution. But nothing is certain in murder trials. Despite Gacy's later denials, obfuscation and finger pointing, there was never really any doubt as to who the killer of those thirty-three young men and boys was. But Gacy had pleaded not guilty by reason of insanity and that would be what the jury needed to consider. That became the prime focus of John Wayne Gacy's fight for life.

And hovering in the background of Gacy's mind, as he awaited trial for his crimes, was the ghost of the domineering father he had loved, hated and been terrified of. Even as cops circled him in December 1978, Gacy had asked an employee to take him to visit his father's grave at Maryhill Cemetery in Niles, Illinois. John Stanley Gacy – the embittered First World War veteran, who had died of cirrhosis of the liver on Christmas Day 1969, while his son served a prison sentence for sodomy in Iowa – had brutalised his sensitive son, and would play a supporting role in unravelling Gacy's personality and revealing his demons at the trial.

The *Chicago Tribune* noted in a piece published on the day before the trial began that none of the seven psychiatrists who had examined Gacy over the preceding fourteen months had diagnosed him with multiple personality disorder. Still, there was other baggage to unpack. Several of the psychiatrists had diagnosed that the contractor's penchant for bondage and sadomasochistic sex with young men was his reaction to the abuse he suffered at the hands of his father.

But the prosecution was adamant that the accused man in the dock was, nevertheless, sane, in full control of his actions and quite simply, evil. Prosecutors had their psychiatric experts as well. Yes, Gacy had an antisocial personality disorder. Yes, he had mental health problems probably as a result of the abuse he endured as a child. But were these issues and a burning rage below the surface reasons for murdering thirty-three times? They argued, no. The prosecution posed the question: 'Would he have committed the crime if a police officer was standing there watching him?'

Both the prosecution and defence painted the clown enthusiast in the most unflattering of terms. The defence admitted he was a psychopath 'motivated by overwhelming and uncontrollable primitive drives.' For the prosecutors, he was 'rational' and just plain 'evil'.

Assistant State Attorney Robert Egan, in his opening address to the jury, outlined the catalogue of monstrous crimes of which Gacy was accused. He told the jurors how Gacy stabbed his first young victim to death and had then gone on to rape, torture and strangle another thirty-two victims. He told them about Gacy's modus operandi – about the 'rope trick' and how he had buried so many victims beneath his own home.

'He started his rampage in 1972 and it took him six years, until 11 December 1978,' an emotional Egan said. In his search for victims, he would head out 'to see what he could pick up at the Greyhound bus station'. Some of the victims, Egan pointed out, were young male sex workers lost in a dangerous world and easy prey for someone like Gacy. Others, such as Godzik and Robert Piest, were suburban kids, who'd been duped into going with Gacy.

'He killed people like he was swatting flies ... [The murders were] planned, mechanical and premeditated.' He pointed out that there was obvious pre-planning on the part of Gacy, such as when he had his young workers dig trenches in his notorious crawl space. Egan said Gacy told cops he had 'wanted to have graves available' for future victims. The court-room veteran also revealed that Gacy had mentioned that his victim, former employee Greg Godzik, had 'dug his own grave'.

The prosecutor also pointed out that there were no blackouts or signs that Gacy was insane when Gacy was finally questioned by Des Plaines detectives. 'He was engaging at times; he laughed at times; he was calm and methodical in his answers,' Egan told the court.

Amirante's partner, Robert Motta, spoke to the jury for more than an hour in laying out what they would hear over the coming weeks from the defence. Motta told them Gacy suffered from an 'unconscious and uncontrollable' mental illness and couldn't be held responsible for his horrific actions. That the crimes occurred 'over and over and over again [showed] a profound and incredible obsession'. 'He sleeps with corpses,' Motta said. 'He lived in a house with bodies under it for years. He was incapable of forming an intent because of a profound mental disease ... his intelligence and thought processes were helpless against a consuming mental disease.'

Motta told the jury the defence would produce four psychiatrists who would testify that John Wayne Gacy was insane, dangerous and should be locked away in an institution forever. Defence shrinks would say that Gacy was: pseudo-neurotic, schizophrenic, paranoid and delusional. 'He's dangerously and incomprehensibly ill,' Motta added.

Prosecutors presented their case first. They shot down the defence contention that Gacy suffered from insanity or multiple personality disorder.

The defence dangled the idea in its opening that Gacy would live out his days in a mental institution. Dr James Cavanaugh, a forensic psychiatrist, pooh-poohed that notion. Gacy simply didn't meet the requirements. 'If the law were followed, he would [eventually] have to be released,' Cavanaugh told the court under questioning by Motta. 'If he were found not guilty by reason of insanity, he would not meet the state's standard for commitment.' The State of Illinois'

Mental Health Code states that 'a person is in need of mental treatment if he suffers from a mental disorder that makes him likely to inflict harm on himself or other persons.' So, it was impossible he told Motta. 'We find it difficult to keep people in mental hospitals who need to be there because of concern … that is a deprivation of their civil rights.' What the defence was suggesting would lead to the inevitable release of Gacy at some point in the future.

Motta suggested the psychiatrist was a 'professional witness for the state'. Cavanaugh was at the time of the trial the director of the Isaac Ray Center at Rush-Presbyterian St. Luke's Hospital which specialised in criminally insane. And Cavanaugh had also been a defence witness on numerous occasions.

Cavanaugh said John Wayne Gacy suffered from a 'mixed personality disorder that has elements of antisocial behaviour, narcissism, obsessive-compulsive behaviour, and, possibly sexual sadism'. But, most importantly, the psychiatrist emphasised: Gacy knew the difference between right and wrong. He was totally sane when he murdered his thirty-three victims.

'Can a man kill thirty-three people over a period of seven years without suffering from a mental disease or defect as defined by Illinois law,' prosecutor Kunkle asked.

Cavanaugh replied: 'I believe he can, and did.'

Cavanaugh went on to reveal the details of an exercise carried out on request by the defence before the trial where Gacy showed his chilling true colours. Gacy was given six ounces of Scotch over a seventy-five minute period and quickly became drunk. Once inebriated, Gacy suggested he and Cavanaugh go out 'cruising' and proceeded to try to leave the hospital. During the episode, John Wayne Gacy was attached to a machine that measures brain waves. No abnormalities as a result of the booze were detected. Gacy was just reverting to his usual behaviour.

The prosecution produced a cast of witnesses, cops and psychiatrists, to give examples of premeditation during Gacy's years of rape, torture and murder. Paramount were the efforts made by Gacy to escape detection from law enforcement, neighbours and friends. The court heard from Cram and Rossi who described how they were asked to dig drainage ditches in Gacy's crawl space, then spread bags of lime. They confirmed that Gacy occasionally looked in the crawl space to ensure they'd followed his instructions to a T.

Cook County Coroner Dr. Robert Stein told the court that the bodies recovered from the house at 8213 West Summerdale Avenue were all 'markedly decomposed [and] putrefied, skeletonised remains'. The young men and boys' agonising deaths were broken down for the court: thirteen died of asphyxiation; six were strangled by ligature; one was stabbed to death; and the cause of death for the remaining ten was listed as 'undetermined'.

The defence argued that all thirty-three of the victims' deaths were caused by accidental erotic asphyxia – they were tragic accidents that occurred during consensual, sadomasochistic sex. Stein scoffed and said that suggestion was 'highly improbable'. While the prosecution's case was straightforward and evidence-driven, the defence would rely on seventeen different witnesses including some of the psychiatrists who had spent time with Gacy since his arrest. No mental-health professional spent more time with Gacy than Dr. Richard Rappaport, who endured sixty-five long hours with the most hated man in America. Rappaport told the court that Gacy had had a fear of being castrated since childhood and that drove him toward a trainload of perversions, including BDSM and other fetishes. His actions were the result of 'irresistible impulses'. The traits he didn't like in himself he projected onto his young victims. He suggested that when Gacy was murdering his victims, in his mind he was killing himself.

'He knew what he was doing when he was squeezing those necks because those victims were himself … [Gacy killed them] to get rid of the hostile, threatening, frightening figures that pervade his conscience. He has to get rid of them, he has to kill them,' the psychiatrist told the court, adding that the murders were 'ritualistic' and a 'cleansing' event for the killer. The murders, he suggested, were the result of psychotic episodes. According to Rappaport's diagnosis, Gacy was a 'borderline personality', somewhere between a neurosis and psychosis. In addition, the patient showed signs of being a paranoid schizophrenic.

The psychiatrist joined the long list of shrinks – amateur and professional – who pointed the finger at the shambolic man's father: the long buried John Stanley Gacy. Gacy Sr. had beaten his son for being a a sissy and 'a queer' when he was a child. He argued that when his father died in 1969, Gacy had been serving time for sodomy in Iowa – and his 'illness' supposedly got worse.

Rappaport emphasised Gacy's fear of castration as part of his traumatic childhood. He suggested Gacy had a sexual interest in his mother. With an Oedipal complex, boys often realise that their mother fixation is 'taboo' he said, and 'little boys imagine the punishment is castration,' he explained. Connected to the desire to possess his mother is a desire to get rid of his father. Rappaport pointed out that this was particularly acute in the case of John Wayne Gacy because of the abuse he suffered at the hands of his father. The young Gacy had tried desperately to please his father but nothing worked, so he would circle back to the fear of castration. The result was 'tremendous homicidal feelings of rage'.

Rappaport also talked about Gacy's personality on the stand. '[Gacy] has a grandiose sense of self. He feels like he's a star. He's the centre of attention. He has a pervasive sense of power and brilliance … that he is entitled to more than the average person,' Rappaport said. 'He had the guards in the County Jail complex in the palm of his hand. He had the wives of the guards bringing him dinner.' A spokesman from the Cook County Department of Corrections later told the *Chicago Sun-Times*: 'Baloney ... No way. Maybe that's what Gacy *told* Rappaport, but there is no way in the world any wife brought him dinner.'

Rappaport also told the court that Gacy had a 'Swiss cheese superego ... [On the surface he might appear normal] but underneath he's cold and ruthless.' He concluded: 'Gacy wore a mask of sanity. In reality it's only a mask ... it covers up the insanity.'

Also testifying on behalf of the defence was victim, Jeffrey Rignall who had been kidnapped, tortured and raped by Gacy in March 1978. Rignall had survived his encounter with Gacy. For some reason, Gacy didn't kill him. On the witness stand, he told the court Gacy could not appreciate his criminality because of the 'beastly and animalistic ways he attacked me.' In short, the violence of the attack on Rignall showed that Gacy was not in control of himself. Under cross-examination Rignall became so overwrought in recalling the details of the attack that he was excused from further testimony.

The defence also called Gacy's seventy-two-year-old mother, Marion, who flew in from North Little Rock, Arkansas, to be by her troubled son's side. 'I love my son,' Marion Gacy told the court. 'I still don't believe any of it. I can't believe it. I can't believe he'd do any of it. Not my son. I'd just like to erase everything.'

Marion Gacy spent a marathon-like twelve hours on the witness stand as she attempted to unravel her son's troubled life. John was a sickly child, 'in and out of hospitals' for the blackouts that plagued his young life. One doctor had suggested his condition was probably epilepsy. During another hospitalisation when he was a teenager, the doctor suggested that her son should receive psychiatric care. Her son would have none of it. 'John pleaded with me: "Mom, don't send me to the psychiatric ward. I'll be good,"' Marion recalled. 'So I went and signed him out, which I probably shouldn't have done.'

As for the relationship between her husband John Stanley and his son – that was a painful matter. She described a tumultuous household where her husband was the violent and abusive head. Marion said that her husband had a 'Jekyll and Hyde' personality. He was 'mean' to his son, frequently called the boy 'stupid' and that he 'seemed to be after him all the time'. Once her husband had thrown his young son against the stove and there were regular beatings with the razor strop. 'My husband didn't show any love and affection for the children. He was very cold-blooded,' Marion said.

Of her son, Marion said, 'He didn't like fighting. John would never lift a hand against him [John Stanley] except to defend me.' She recalled that, after giving birth to Gacy's younger sister Karen, her husband punched 'her right square in the face with his fist' as her terrified children screamed. She also detailed her son's litany of medical maladies and nascent perversions. Once she could not find any of her fine silk underwear: 'He [her son] had them all in a brown paper bag under the porch with him.'

Booze possessed her husband. When he drank, a perfectly lovely, reasonable man became a maniac. The problem was that he drank *every* day – fighting to keep the horrors he had witnessed in the First World War at bay. 'He'd come home from work and the first thing [he would do was] he would go down in the basement. He'd come up and he was pretty well under [drunk],' she testified while fighting back tears. 'He would talk and then he would answer himself, and it would be two different voices. I always called him a Jekyll and Hyde.' But when he wasn't boozing, she insisted, 'he was the best person in the world.'

When John Stanley Gacy died on Christmas Day 1969 and prison officials refused to let John attend the funeral, 'That made it worse for him,' Marion told the court. She went on to add that when he was sprung from prison in 1971 and she lived briefly with him at the notorious house on Summerdale Avenue, 'John was always helping me. He was always very good to me.'

If Marion Gacy's testimony was designed to evoke some level of sympathy for her son, it worked – to a point. It was one of the few times that John Wayne Gacy exhibited an iota of emotion during the harrowing five-week trial. Just before a recess was called by Judge Louis Garippo, Gacy was allowed to give his sobbing mother a hug.

The defence also called Gacy's younger sister Karen Kuzma, two years his junior. On her relationship with her brother, she said, 'We fought like cats and dogs sometimes, but I'd be there for him and he was always there for me.' Motta asked point blank: 'Is your brother, John Wayne Gacy, evil?' 'No way. The brother that I know is always sweet, loving, understanding, generous,' Kuzma answered. And, when asked about the relationship between the rest of the family and their father, she answered, 'Very stormy.' She too described the old man as a 'Jekyll and Hyde' character.

Karen recollected for the court that, after a particularly brutal beating, John Stanley called his son a 'coward' and threatened to kill the boy. 'He said: "Hit me. You will never stick up for yourself. Hit me,"' Kuzma recalled through her tears. 'Dad was just never pleased with how John was. I think he wanted John to be like him, and John was not bad. No one ever praised him. My dad never once said to my brother, "Hey, John, you really did good for a change."' Their father would even call Gacy's childhood friends 'fairies and queers' Kuzma said.

Another surviving victim of Gacy, Donald Voorhees, who was raped by Gacy in 1967 in Waterloo, Iowa was called by the prosecution. Like Rignall, Voorhees was also traumatised to a severe degree and abruptly stopped on the witness stand, and could not continue.

Another Gacy survivor, Robert Donnelly, described being raped by Gacy in December 1977. At times, he was clearly distressed and struggled to carry on. He appeared on the verge of breaking down. Gacy kept laughing at the terrorised young man as Donnelly testified. Defence lawyer Robert Motta tried to shake the victim from his testimony on cross-examination but could not.

Mostly, during testimony, Gacy appeared unmoved by the heartbreaking and often gruesome accounts. But, for the second time in the trial, John Wayne Gacy became emotional when his second wife, Carole Hoff (now Lofgren), was called to the witness stand. As Lofgren – who was married to Gacy for three-and-a-half years – took the stand, Gacy looked down at the floor, broke down and sobbed. 'I feel sorry for him. My heart goes out to him,' the pretty thirty-five-year-old told the court, as she too began sobbing.

She told the court she had not seen her ex-husband for two years. She described a different Gacy from the animal who coldly snuffed out so many young lives. 'He was a warm, understanding person,' Lofgren testified. 'He was very easy to talk to. He knew a lot of things. I met a lot of interesting people through John … He was a very smart, brilliant man. He had a memory like an elephant … He was a very good father to my girls. They called him "Daddy" even before our marriage, they still refer to him as their dad.'

But there were some unusual things about her husband, Carole admitted – and the house on Summerdale where they had all resided. After the couple married on 1 July 1972, Lofgren said she noticed a peculiar odour in the home 'and it just kept getting stronger and stronger.' She kept asking her husband about the stench and wondered if they perhaps had a problem with mice and some of them had maybe died under the floor. Then there were the gnats. 'He [Gacy] said there was a pipe broken or cracked and it was leaking. He said the dampness was causing the smell. He told me I shouldn't bother to call an exterminator – he would take care of it,' Lofgren recalled. She too noted that her husband would occasionally put a bag of lime in the crawl space.

Again, the overwhelming shadow of John Stanley Gacy raised its head in Carole's testimony. She said she had seen her former husband cry around Christmas because he 'missed his father', who had died during the holidays eleven years before.

As for Gacy's sexual preferences and peccadilloes, Lofgren told Sam Amirante: 'He told me he was bisexual. At first, I didn't know what a bisexual was. I just didn't make anything of it. It didn't make any difference to me.' And besides, their sex life – while it lasted – was good and she described her former husband as 'very gentle, very warm' in bed. But soon, she admitted, he began to lose interest in having sex before, finally, on Mother's Day 1975, he announced that a recent intimate encounter would be their last. 'I couldn't believe it coming from John,' she said.

She recalled a time after they had divorced in the spring of 1978, when they had tried to have sex. Gacy couldn't do it. 'We tried to start to make love and John broke down. He said he was afraid he was going more the other way,' Lofgren said. 'I held him and we cried. I said, "I can't be with you every minute of the day. I'll help you anyway I can but you have to help yourself."'

As for his sordid past and criminal conviction in Iowa, Gacy had told his wife it was a pornography beef and involved young boys and she believed him. It had all been a mistake. Gacy frequently left their house at one a.m. saying he was going to check on some construction project or the other. Once, she waited up for him. When he got back to the house and saw she was awake, he looked startled. Gacy told his wife he had come home to get something but left without whatever it was he was after. In the passenger seat of Gacy's car, as he drove away, Lofgren testified she saw a young, blond-haired boy.

Life with Gacy was a whirlwind. He was a workaholic and always busy. 'We were lucky if we found time to go out on occasion for dinner or dancing. I think John could go on an hour of sleep, maybe less,' Lofgren testified. And the late nights were taking a toll during the final eighteen months of their marriage. Lofgren told her husband he should slow down. He reassured her: 'That's all right. I'm going to die at the age of forty anyway. Then you'll have everything.' Lofgren added: 'He said it would be a violent death.'

As for an insanity plea? 'I think he's been sane the whole time I've known him,' Carole said.

By the fifth week of the trial, Gacy was unhappy with how things were going. He wrote a letter to Judge Louis Garippo claiming that he didn't approve of the insanity plea his team had entered. He also did not like his lawyers forbidding him from taking the witness stand as he wanted to and the defence had not called enough medical witnesses. In addition to this the cops were lying in regard to the verbal statements he made to them after he was arrested. He wanted it declared a mistrial.

Garippo was firm and informed Gacy that both defence and prosecution had been given ample time and funds to secure the witnesses they required. He also informed him that it was up to him if he wanted to testify. The matter quickly fizzled out.

On 11 March 1978, final arguments began. Prosecutor Terry Sullivan outlined a laundry list of the lives taken by Gacy, the sexual abuse he had carried out of young men like Voorhees, Donnelly and Rignall and the lengths he had gone to in order to avoid detection. He addressed the jury: 'John Gacy has accounted for more human devastation than many earthly catastrophes, but one must tremble. I tremble when thinking about just how close he came to getting away with it all.' Sullivan described the survivors who had testified against him as the 'living dead' and Gacy as the 'worst of all murderers'.

After Sullivan's four-hour closing, Sam Amirante delivered the defence's closing arguments. He disputed Cavanaugh's testimony on Gacy's sanity, instead focusing on the psychiatrists who spoke for the defence. Amirante also took aim at Sullivan's closing for not including germane information that had been presented at trial. The diminutive attorney even accused prosecutors of arousing hatred of his client. He reiterated the argument that Gacy was a 'man driven by compulsions he was unable to control', referring specifically to his psychiatric experts – and the testimony of Jeffrey Rignall, a survivor of one of Gacy's sexual frenzies. The state, Amirante said, had not met its burden of truth. He asked the jury to render a verdict of not guilty by reason of insanity. Gacy, Amirante said, was a danger to himself and the public and making his client the focus of psychological study would be a benefit to society and science.

Coming back to counter the defence's closing statements, Prosecutor William Kunkle called the defence's argument of insanity, 'a sham'. Gacy controlled his actions, and he planned his crimes and their cover-up. The veteran prosecutor said Gacy had shown he could murder without remorse. Psychiatric treatment would be of no benefit to him, he said, citing the 1968 report on the contractor that had been drawn up when he was arrested on a charge of sodomy in Waterloo, Iowa. If those dire warnings in that report had been heeded, Kunkle said, Gacy would not have been freed, thirty-three people would still be alive and they would not be in the Chicago courthouse for this trial.

Kunkle finished his closing statement in a dramatic fashion. Photos of the twenty-two victims who had been identified were displayed on a board in the court-room. Also entered into evidence was the trap door from Gacy's crawl space at Summerdale Avenue.

'Don't show sympathy to the accused,' Kunkle told the jury, as he slowly removed every one of the twenty-two photos from the board, 'show justice.' He moved towards the trap door clutching the photos of Gacy's named victims. 'Show the same sympathy this man showed when he took these lives and put them there,' Kunkle said, as he opened the trap door and tossed the photos through the opening.

The jury for the trial of John Wayne Gacy deliberated for less than two hours. And when they returned with their verdict, they announced they had found the Killer Clown guilty of thirty-three counts of murder, along with sexual assault and taking indecent liberties with a child (Robert Piest).

In 1980, it was the most murder convictions of any single American killer.

18

A Date with Death

On 13 March 1980, the jury again retired after finding him guilty of murder in the first degree thirty-three times to decide on the sentencing. It took them two hours and fifteen minutes to decide the convicted serial killer's fate. At 6.30 p.m. Central Standard Time, they returned to the court-room with their decision. The court clerk made the announcement to the hushed room: 'The court shall sentence John Wayne Gacy to death.' John Wayne Gacy would die in the Illinois electric chair.

The *Tribune* later reported that after the jury announced the death sentence and made their way out of the court-room, many broke down in tears. According to the *Chicago Sun-Times*, family and friends of the victims and survivors of Gacy gasped and then broke into applause when the sentence was announced. They were soon hushed by court-room officers. Gacy, dressed in a green three-piece suit, was expressionless. His execution date was set for 2 June 1980.

Judge Louis Garripo also became emotional as he thanked the jury for its service. He said he did not know what the trial cost taxpayers but it was a small price to pay for justice.

Later, with the bombastic businessman's personal stamp, Gacy summoned prosecutor William Kunkle to the courthouse lock-up. He wanted to congratulate the man who had just sent him to death row. Kunkle later told reporters what Gacy said, and quoted him: 'I have no hard feelings toward you or your team. You were just doing your job. I can accept the guilty verdict, but I don't think they should have given me the death penalty, based on my mental state. I think it was God's will. All the jury did was to do the same thing I have been trying to do to myself for the last ten years: Destroy myself.'

Kunkle had responded: 'John, all you've got left is to try and make peace with yourself.'

After the trial ended, 'Many of the policemen and investigators and the prosecution team went over to a little place called Jeans ... a watering hole on 26th Street,' Kunkle recalled. 'One of the jurors wanted to come too. Sure enough, around ten o'clock, after the jurors had packed up and had one last dinner together, he called over to the bar and we sent two investigators to pick him up and he drank with us until four in the morning. Then we had another investigator drive him home.'

Gacy's lawyer, Sam Amirante, vowed to keep fighting for his client's life.

The next day, 14 March 1980, Gacy was transferred to the infamous Joliet Penitentiary, thirty miles south-west of Chicago, for a slew of medical tests before the last stop: death row at Stateville Penitentiary. There, Gacy would join twenty-two other doomed men.

While America's most notorious and prolific killer had been sentenced to die, his execution date was not set in stone. Illinois law dictates that any death sentence is automatically stayed while an appeal is made to the state's supreme court. Executions in America are seldom done-and-dusted affairs. As a case winds through the appeal process it can take years or even decades to dispatch a condemned prisoner to the hereafter.

Gacy, now thirty-eight, didn't stay long at Joliet. He was bound for southern Illinois and the Menard Correctional Center – within sight of the Mississippi River, although only for some of the inmates. Menard – perhaps best known as the birthplace of the creator of cartoon character Popeye, Elzie Crisler Segar – is in tiny Chester, Illinois, which has a population of 5,800, and it is a long way from Chicago. The town is closer to St Louis, Missouri, than the Windy City. There are almost as many inmates in the prison as there are inhabitants in the town.

In his windowless cell, Gacy was the first death-row inmate, though he would soon be joined by more condemned men. 'The State decided that the first guy who got the death penalty after the beginning of the year in 1980 they were going to send here, and that was me,' Gacy told *The New Yorker* magazine many years later. 'When they brought me down here, the press came out with how I was scared to be with the prison population, so they put me here by myself. Like the State was going to be concerned with my feelings.'

In prison, Gacy packed on more weight and waited as his lawyers appealed his death sentence. Guards in the sprawling prison called him 'J. W. Gacy' and, once in a while, 'Chester the Molester'. While he was physically alone most of the time, the serial killer was flooded with letters from the curious, kooks and, remarkably, people who believed he was innocent.

After his trial, Gacy became the killer that most fascinated and horrified America, surpassing even Charles Manson. Numerous books and articles were written about him as the country grappled with the idea of the monster who slaughtered thirty-three young men and boys and how he got away with it for so long. What drove him? What the hell was wrong with him? How did this happen?

He was the most notorious man in America but Gacy didn't even like other convicts talking about him. 'When I first walked in here [prison], I was scared to death. I didn't know how to think like a con: it wasn't part of my nature, and I still can't do it,' Gacy told *The New Yorker* in later years. 'I didn't realise men could be bitches. Women sit at home and gossip, but in prison I've learned that as soon as you walk away they'll talk about you. Everybody who doesn't say a word when you're standing there will put in his two cents when you're gone. They get bigger balls when you're not around.'

But Gacy's status as the pre-eminent serial killer meant more physical dangers awaited him in prison. Sticking Gacy would give a fellow convict instant credibility. And on 15 February 1983, Henry Brisbon, a fellow death-row inmate tried to do just that. Brisbon, twenty-seven at the time, was best known as the I-57 killer. He had murdered a Chicago businessman named James Schmidt and his fiancée Dorothy Cerny on the side of the highway near the Second City in 1973, when he was just seventeen years old. While awaiting trial at Menard, Brisbon had stabbed a fellow jailbird named Ronald Morgan to death, earning himself a date with the electric chair. There was no apparent motive behind the murder. After he was sentenced to fry for the Morgan murder, Brisbon exploded in court: 'You'll never get me. I'll kill again. Then you'll have another long trial. And then I'll do it again.'

One day, whilst on a voluntary work programme in the prison, Brisbon slipped out of his handcuffs, broke away from a death-row guard and, using a piece of sharpened wire, stabbed Gacy and another inmate, William Jones. Gacy was stabbed in the arm and he and Jones both survived. The death penalty in Illinois was eventually put on ice in 2007 and Brisbon remains caged but still alive.

As the decade wore on, Gacy's lawyer Sam Amirante continued working on his appeal. Gacy himself was keenly interested in the law and read a slew of legal books. The Killer Clown also began filing a blizzard of paper, motions and appeals. One of his biggest contentions was that the search warrant granted to Des Plaines detectives on 13 December 1978 was invalid. He also, again, took issue with his lawyers' insanity plea at his blockbuster trial. Despite the mountain of evidence, Gacy still mainained his innocence. His efforts went nowhere though. In the middle of 1984, the Supreme Court of Illinois upheld Gacy's conviction and confirmed his execution by lethal injection now scheduled for 14 November 1984.

Gacy filed another appeal. It was denied by the Supreme Court of the United States on 4 March 1985. The next year, he petitioned for a new trial. His latest lawyer, Richard Kling, argued that Gacy's defence team was 'ineffective' at his first trial. That gambit was also dismissed on 11 September 1986.

Gacy continued to fight. He appealed the 1985 court decision that he should be executed. That was torpedoed by the Illinois Supreme Court on 29 September 1988. A new date was set for his execution: 11 January 1989. All Gacy had left was the knowledge that he would die in the electric chair.

The monotony of prison began to wear John Wayne Gacy down. 'Prison life has been the doldrums, same goddamn thing day after day,' Gacy moaned to writer Alec Wilkinson for an article in *The New Yorker* in 1994. He was stuck in a tiny cell without windows. Death row denizens were only let out for a few hours a week. Three showers per week were allowed. 'I don't know if it's night or day. I can't tell you if it's raining. Being in prison is like being in Las Vegas, where you're gambling and you don't know what's going on outside. I was a workaholic outside anyway, so time meant nothing to me then, either,' Gacy added.

He continued his nighthawk ways, going to bed anywhere from two-thirty to four a.m. Then he would get up at five a.m. for breakfast. Gacy still didn't need much sleep.

As for hitting the barbells and exercise, that was for the other mooks, Gacy said. Instead, he would go to the recreation room and play cards with other residents of death row before answering his letters. 'Personally, if I was on the outside I'd never write someone in prison,' Gacy told Wilkinson. Fans would send him paintings of clowns, devil figurines and T-shirts. These 'gifts' were declined at the prison gate. Cons were only allowed to receive letters and books. 'But no novels on homosexuality, bestiality or incest. They say it stimulates you,' Gacy said, adding that skin magazines like *Penthouse* and *Playboy* were allowed. 'They show lesbian films on the late-night, in-house channel – two women getting it on, that's not supposed to incite you. We're not on the farm down here, so I can't understand where the bestiality comes in.'

Always well-organised and fastidious, Gacy also kept a detailed logbook while on death row. 'I log day to day. Every meal, every phone call, every movement – I log it,' he told CBS News.

As he awaited his fate, Gacy did develop a passion for painting. He began to paint with a fervour he once reserved for construction, bullshitting and murder. Gacy's colourful canvases were inspired by a wide array of objects. He painted famed 1930s gangster John Dillinger, Jesus Christ, birds, skulls and his old home on Summerdale Avenue. But mostly he painted clowns – including a slew of self-portraits in his jester alter egos, Pogo and Patches. Gacy cited Walt Disney as his 'mentor' and claimed his paintings brought 'joy into people's lives'. Indeed, they became instant collectibles despite and perhaps because of their often grotesque imagery. Gacy was even allowed to make money from the sale of the paintings until 1985 when Illinois pulled the plug on the art scam. But afterwards, he kept painting and even said of his portrait of Christ, 'I see him as myself.' Still to this day, the paintings are frequently displayed at exhibitions, others have been sold for considerable amounts of cash at auction. Prices have ranged from as low as $200 to a whopping $20,000.

Gacy bristled when CBS compared him to Milwaukee's cannibal serial killer, Jeffrey Dahmer when he was arrested in 1991 and went on trial in 1992. Dahmer had raped and murdered seventeen young men. Dahmer's defence team had also called for a 'not guilty by reason of insanity' verdict. The jury found him guilty. 'What do I think of Jeffrey Dahmer? I don't know the man personally, but I'll tell you this: it's a good example of why insanity doesn't belong in the court-room because if Jeffrey Dahmer doesn't meet the requirements for insanity, I'd hate to hell to run into the guy that does,' Gacy told the TV network. 'I hate it when they put me in the same club as them [other serial killers].'

Gacy spent most of his time on death row continuing to claim he was innocent – mostly – of the sex murders of the thirty-three boys, many of them buried beneath his house. He even began baulking at the idea he was a serial killer – a murderer, sure, but not a serial killer. Most condemned men – and a few women – at some point realise the inevitability of their executions and they make peace with themselves and their fate. Not Gacy. He did not want to die in the electric chair and he would do all he could to avoid it.

In a series of interviews with Wilkinson for *The New Yorker* magazine in 1993 and 1994, Gacy – his hair now snow-white and his skin pale, spoke of the dreariness of his life on death row. 'I go to bed and say three "Hail Mary"'s and the "Our Father". I dream about the life I used to have. I dream about being in construction. I dreamt one night that my daughter was getting married and of all the things that I would do for her,' he told the magazine.

In the bombshell interviews, Gacy also began constructing the premise that he was innocent and that others had murdered the victims and pinned it on him. Somehow, they had managed to bury twenty-seven people in the crawl space of his home without him knowing. It was a theory he warmed to. 'For a while, I would tape newspaper pictures of the victims to the wall beside my bed and go to sleep seeing if I would dream about them or if I could recall if I ever met them. I would look at them and say, "Who the hell are you, and how did you die?" I don't have fantasy-type dreams, and I don't ever have nightmares,' Gacy said.

One of the most bizarre oddities of Gacy's claim to innocence was what he called his 'Victims Book'. The article for *The New Yorker* revealed that, in the late eighties, Gacy began corresponding with a man who fervently believed in his innocence and was researching Gacy's case. The man was referred to as Chris Lewis in the article although that was not his real name. In his first letter to Lewis, Gacy claimed he didn't know who murdered at least thirty-two of the victims. In fact, Gacy said he didn't even know who the boys were, or their backgrounds.

'I wanted to know who the hell these guys were,' Gacy told Alec Wilkinson of *The New Yorker*, 'because, keep it in mind, at the trial they were all boy scouts and altar boys, and I was the monster that came along and swatted them like flies. Jesus, I didn't even want to run into myself the way they described me.

'My idea is, if I didn't kill them, and I had no knowledge of them, then who did they know? If I didn't do the murders, then we have to find out who did them by finding out about the victims and cross-referencing them. Did any of them know each other? If you can't find the who, what and why, where are you going to go with it?'

Lewis was nothing if not fanatical in his belief in Gacy. Together the pair had compiled newspaper clippings, interviews, photos, legal papers and more. He took photos of where the boys had worked, called their relatives or wrote to them and put the information in a folder for his new friend. According to Wilkinson's article, the Gacy brief was 'larger than the Manhattan telephone book'. It was entitled 'Victims Research: Confidential'. Inside, it was divided into thirty-three sections – one for each of Gacy's victims – and further divided into the order in which their bodies were found.

Where the identity of the victim was known a section kicked off with a photo of that boy. With those that still had unidentified remains there was a police reconstruction. It also featured a description of how each victim was murdered and where the body was found. Lewis wrote long reports on what he discovered about the victims, including names of their pets, photos of their homes – literally every cough and spit about the victims' short, tragic lives. An additional touch on some sections was a crude, hand-drawn design of a red-spoked wheel that indicated Gacy was away from Chicago at the time of their disappearance.

According to Alec Wilkinson, Gacy referred to himself in the third person when explaining the complicated charts and formulas of murder from this book. 'Gacy went out of town,' he said. 'When did Gacy leave? Gacy generally went out of town on a Sunday.'

'This is years of solid research, chasing down leads,' Gacy told the reporter. 'Everybody wants this. I'm not leaving it to anybody. I'm giving it to my sister with instructions to destroy it. People ask what would I do if I got free, and I tell them I'm still obsessed with this case. They say, "What the hell? Why do you care what happened to them?" and I say, "Because I want to know what happened as much as anyone else. If *I* don't get justice, then how will the victims?"'

The convicted killer asked how could someone so 'family oriented' like himself be a killer? There was no motive for him, he insisted. If he was going to be executed for their murders, he should know something about the people he was supposed to have killed. 'God damn, if you're going to kill me, let me know what it's for. Even if I didn't kill somebody, I want to know what the hell happened. If I'm going to kill somebody, why did I kill them? The why, the when and the how. What happened on Summerdale? Right now, we don't know what happened on Summerdale.'

He conceded that while he had 'some knowledge' of five of the murders (McCoy, Butkovich, Godzik, Szyc and Piest) the other twenty-eight homicides had been committed by his employees, David Cram and Michael Rossi. They had keys to his house. They murdered those boys while he was away on business trips, Gacy posited. They put the bodies in the crawl space. In 1977, he said that Cram and Rossi had asked him to hire a friend who was connected to a man who ran a sex ring – supplying boys to older men. The boys were murdered because they were members of the ring and involved in making snuff films and they wanted to quit.

Gacy and his acolyte Lewis spun a tantalising yarn but it didn't stand up. Gacy had started killing young men in 1972 – well before he claims Cram and Rossi became involved. Also, it was impossible to believe that every single one of Gacy's victims were involved in sex work. Despite Gacy's extensive efforts and help from Lewis, nothing could stop the clock on his march towards oblivion. The 1980s had ebbed into the 1990s and Gacy's myriad efforts – from the fanboy researcher to innumerable appeals – all hit a brick wall.

Gacy's crimes made the small screen in 1992, with the two-part made-for-TV film *To Catch a Killer*, starring fabulous character actor Brian Dennehy as Gacy and Michael Riley as Des Plaines Lieutenant Joseph Kozenczak. Some of the names in the film were fictionalised. It isn't known if Gacy ever saw the film.

He had other concerns by that point. Death had a date and it would not be missed.

'I'll tell you what – I'm not going to make no damn Ted Bundy last-minute confessions,' Gacy told Alec Wilkinson toward the end of the interview with *The New Yorker*. 'None of that shit. I'm not going to put my family through the media circus. And I'm not going to be buried with my mother and father, like some people have written, because I don't want no one desecrating their graves.'

Until the bitter end, Gacy would not stop fighting for his life. As time crawled on, he became more and more convinced of his innocence. It was the piston that drove him. In October 1993, the United States Supreme Court – the highest court in the land – rejected John Wayne Gacy's final appeal. The Illinois Supreme Court set another execution date for 10 May 1994. Even ardent opponents of the death penalty raised nary a peep for the Killer Clown. Most people just shrugged and used the old American chestnut that John Wayne Gacy was a poster boy for the death penalty. If anyone deserved it, it was Gacy. And they would have their pound of flesh.

19

The End

By the spring of 1994, the end was rapidly approaching for John Wayne Gacy. The serial-killer clown who snuffed out the lives of at least thirty-three young men and boys was about to pay for his sinister crimes.

On Monday 9 May 1994, Gacy was transferred from his home of fourteen years on Illinois' death row at the Menard Correctional Center, back home to the Stateville Correctional Center in Crest Hill on the outskirts of the south-western suburbs of Chicago. He carted boxes of legal papers with him and was still filing appeals against the death sentence until his final hours. His appeals were rejected.

Gacy insisted he wasn't afraid to die. 'If you've believed you have lived your life the right way then you do not have nothing to fear,' he told CBS News. He was asked if he was afraid of meeting his maker. 'No. I'm fairly comfortable with Him,' the doomed killer said. 'I've been under the service of the priest for the last ten years. I have no qualms about doing that. I've had confession. I've had communion and I am at peace with myself.'

The final afternoon of his life was a respite from his dreary existence at Menard. He was allowed a final meal – a picnic in the grounds of the prison with his family. Ironically, for his final meal, the former contractor ordered a bucket of Kentucky Fried Chicken, a dozen deep-fried shrimp, French fries, fresh strawberries and a Diet Coke.

In the weeks before he was executed, Gacy had moaned to writer Alec Wilkinson that it was unfair that his family was not allowed to attend his execution. 'The prison won't let me have my family there – I hear the victims' families can come (this wasn't actually the case), but I can't have my own family,' Gacy said. 'I don't know. And I'm not going to invite anyone else, either. I got all these people that tell me they want to be there, and they say, "I've known you for eight years, you've got to let me come," but I spent my life as a workaholic and a loner and I'll go out that way, too.'

One of those who planned to be on hand to watch the life ebb out of Gacy was prosecutor William Kunkle. 'It'll provide closure. The families of the victims won't be allowed into the viewing room and I feel I should be there as their representative, and also as a representative of law enforcement,' Kunkle told *The Chicago Tribune* on the day Gacy would die. 'It's my obligation as a prosecutor. If you're going to send someone to his death it's appropriate you're there to see it. And I do not have a personal animosity toward John or a personal desire to see him dead.'

On his final evening of life, Gacy, raised as a Roman Catholic, said prayers with a priest.

Outside the prison, anti-death-penalty activists, holding a candlelight vigil, were shouted down by a crowd of 1,000 that wanted to see Gacy dead as a doornail. Some even wore T-shirts alluding to the serial killer's previous persona as a community entertainer. The shirts read: 'No tears for the clown'.

In addition to an unusually large number of officials, there were twelve media representatives at the execution for a total of forty-one witnesses. Just before 12.40 a.m., Gacy was wheeled on a gurney into the death chamber. By 1994, Illinois was executing prisoners by lethal injection replacing the ancient electric chair that had dispatched so many killers to oblivion.

Officials started almost immediately to prepare the doomed murderer for the ritual of death. Howard Peters III, the head of the Illinois Department of Corrections, spoke with Gacy before the drugs were administered. The serial killer insisted again that what was about to unfold was unjust. 'He said taking his life would not compensate for the loss of the others and this was a mistake,' Peters told reporters. 'He said taking his life was basically murdering him.'

And then came the final words consummate bullshitter John Wayne Gacy would ever utter. He told officials in the death house: 'Kiss my ass.'

Death would be brought about by administering a three-drug cocktail. The rotund, fifty-two-year-old Gacy was given an injection of sodium pentothal first. 'The reaction was like he was going to sleep,' Peters said. 'He closed his eyes and took a deep breath.' But state-prison officials fouled up when the second drug – a muscle relaxant – was injected into the condemned man's arm. Experts later said it was unlikely the malfunction caused Gacy any discomfort or pain. But, as a precaution, the blinds to the death chamber were suddenly pulled down. The knockout punch was still to come. Pancuronium bromide flowed, stopping Gacy's heart. And, when the blinds were opened again, the man who had terrorised Chicago was still, his pasty skin now purple. Gacy was pronounced dead at 12.58 a.m. It had taken eighteen minutes for him to die.

'He got a much easier death than any of his victims,' William Kunkle said.

Cook County Sheriff's investigator Greg Bedoe, told the *Chicago Tribune*, 'It finally dawned on him that it was over. This game he was playing, this dual life he was leading, was finally exposed. But he still thought he could call the shots.' Bedoe was there when Gacy confessed to police in 1978. He recalled after his death that, 'He was like, "Okay, we're going to clear up thirty-some murders." He was smoking cigars and he was the centre of attention, with six or seven people interviewing him. In his mind that made him a big deal. Mr. Big Shot. He never showed any emotion. I cannot emphasise this enough: He has never, in my dealings with him, showed one ounce of remorse or sorrow or sympathy.' Bedoe was also watching Gacy when Gacy was sentenced to the ultimate punishment: 'I was standing to the left of Judge Garippo when he sentenced Gacy to die. I could look him straight in the eye. He didn't blink.'

The families of the victims were relieved following Gacy's execution. A number had requested to see Gacy die, but they had been turned down. About two dozen of them gathered outside the Stateville Correctional Center waiting for confirmation of his death. But they wondered why it had taken so long for justice to be served. 'This should have happened a long time ago,' said Tim Neider the brother of eighteen-year-old James Mowry. 'I'm just glad a little justice was finally done here.'

Eugenia Godzik, the sister of Greg Godzik, was bitter that Gacy had lived two decades longer than her brother. She told reporters she wanted more from the relatively uneventful execution. 'I wish he could have suffered more,' she said. 'The punishment didn't fit the crime.'

Gacy's body was cremated as per his wishes but not before his brain was removed and sent to the University of Chicago where it would be examined. One of the questions on the minds of researchers was whether the head injury he had suffered as a result of the accident with the swing when he was eleven had damaged his brain and triggered the pathology that led this seemingly normal man – one who presented as a pillar of the community – to kill?

The case of Charles Whitman was one of the rare instances where something in a killer's brain could have correlated with their evil actions. Whitman had nested in a bell tower at the University of Texas in August 1966 from where he proceeded to kill twelve people and wound another thirty-three with a sniper rifle. Following his demise, an examination of his brain revealed he was suffering from a brain tumour. Even then, researchers could not definitively link the tumour to the murders though.

One expert was doubtful an examination and study of Gacy's brain would reveal anything remotely profound. 'People have come up empty-handed, whether positive or negative,' said Dr. Mauro Dal Canto of the Northwestern University Medical Center. 'I doubt that we're going to find anything that is specific or peculiar to this guy. This is just a sick individual, but a sickness of the mind in general doesn't have a morphological [physical] counterpart.' The test took an hour and as Dal Canto predicted, it showed nothing.

Dr. Eric D. Caine, a professor of psychiatry and neurology at the University of Rochester, told the *Chicago Tribune* that psychiatric disorders do not have the markers of dementia and other neurological illnesses. 'When you get to psychiatric disorders, you don't have a nice marker like from a stroke showing in an autopsy saying, "Here I am,"' Caine explained. 'There's not a literature on the brains of very bad people. As for serial killers, fortunately, there aren't a lot of them, so there isn't a comparison between them and a group of normal people.'

Still, researchers were hopeful they would get to the nub of 'what parts of the brain are involved in aggressive criminal behaviour'.

University of Western Ontario criminology professor Michael Arntfield asserted that Gacy's horrendous childhood didn't necessarily create a killer either. 'Upbringings aren't necessarily deterministic, they are correlated with certain antisocial traits later in life,' Arntfield said. 'That's why we see serial killers, particularly sex killers, have common characteristics in their childhoods. Itinerant, move frequently, they don't form social bonds, they have parents who are physically or emotionally abusive or have addiction issues. This collective trauma is dealt with by resilient people who go on to remove themselves from that outlet and find positive outlets later in life. But when ingredient X is added, the mixture is highly combustible. With someone with sexual proclivities plus trauma plus antisocial tendencies – you have a dangerous cocktail there when all the ingredients line up for a violent serial predator.'

The murders, investigation, trial and execution of Gacy exacted a profound toll on the participants. William Kunkle later went into private practice, Judge Louis Garippo resigned from the bench and also returned to private practice. The lives of the victims' families as well as the victims themselves, were forever changed and often shattered beyond repair. Fathers and mothers died young. Some siblings became drug addicts, others ended up dead.

James Pickell was the first Des Plaines detective assigned to the case when fifteen-year-old Robert Piest disappeared on 11 December 1978. It was Pickell – a young father of five – who linked Gacy's 1968 sodomy conviction and reported assaults in Chicago to the contractor's involvement in the boy's disappearance. Pickell took Gacy's first statements. He spent hours tailing Gacy, checking his background and interviewing him. Although Pickell would tell his family little of the horrors that flooded his consciousness during that time, it took a toll. 'My father was obsessed and terrified,' his daughter Cindy later told the *Tribune*. 'He often told my mother that he could imagine his son being one of the victims. Our family went to Florida for Christmas 1979, and it was there we really noticed my father was not his usual fun-loving, happy-go-lucky self. He was short-tempered and had lost quite a bit of weight,' Cindy recalled. Several months later, the dedicated cop was diagnosed with diabetes. Doctors told the family it was likely triggered by stress. On 28 May 1980 – after Gacy had been convicted and sentenced to death – Pickell suffered a fatal heart attack, while mowing the lawn of his suburban home. He was just forty-one years old.

Des Plaines cops agreed that the detective's shocking death was a result of his work on the Killer Clown investigation. 'My father was Gacy's thirty-fourth victim,' Cindy Pickell said.

But even now, decades after the serial killer was executed, a slew of questions remain. John Wayne Gacy – long settled in hell – is not through with us yet.

20

Unanswered Questions

John Wayne Gacy had told some detectives in Des Plaines and Chicago that his death tally could be as high as forty-five. After his trial, Gacy also told anyone who would listen that two of his employees – Cram and Rossi – were the true killers. Decades on from 1978 when he was arrested, those questions continue to haunt survivors and the public at large. Theories continue to emerge about this unfathomably dark chapter in the history of the Windy City. Did Gacy have accomplices in carrying out his vile deeds? And were there more victims that the Killer Clown didn't tell cops about?

Former Des Plaines detective Mike Arendt, who was involved in the surveillance, interrogation and arrest of Gacy, doesn't believe there are more victims out there. 'He was such a loudmouth,' Arendt said, 'he couldn't help himself blabbing it out. He would have told detectives. There are no other bodies, I don't think. I think he would've told us at that time because he was a braggart.'

Yet Gacy told detectives that he had thrown *five* bodies in the river. Cops only recovered four bodies. What about the fifth? Gacy had smirked: 'That's for you guys to find out.'

Employees of Gacy had a nasty habit of disappearing. Some ended up dead in his crawl space or dumped into the Des Plaines River. One such young man was twenty-five-year-old Charles Antonio Hattula, who disappeared on 13 May 1978. On 23 May 1978, Hattula was discovered drowned in the Pecatonica River near Freeport, Illinois. By that point, Gacy's crypt in his crawl space was full and he had begun dumping his victims' bodies into the rivers around Chicago. Hattula was an employee of P. D. M.

It was Michael Rossi who told detectives investigating Gacy of Hattula's death and Godzik's disappearance. Rossi told cops that it was no secret that Hattula and Gacy had quarrelled. When their co-worker failed to show up for work, Gacy had actually told his team that Hattula had drowned. When investigators contacted cops in Freeport they were informed that Hattula had fallen to his death from a bridge. The death was officially ruled as asphyxia by drowning. Des Plaines detectives then put the kibosh on the theory that Hattula was another of the Killer Clown's victims.

And what about the years when there were no recorded Gacy murders? John Wayne Gacy's first recorded murder occurred on 3 January 1972, when he stabbed to death sixteen-year-old Timothy Jack McCoy after picking him up at the Greyhound bus station downtown. The killer then appeared to take a three-and-a-half year hiatus, and was dormant until the summer of 1975, when he murdered eighteen-year-old P. D. M. employee John Butkovich.

Cold-case and serial-killer expert Michael Arntfield, a criminology professor at the University of Western Ontario and one of the founders of the Murder Accountability Project, said there's a definite possibility there are more Gacy victims. 'When we look at the disposal pathway modus operandi of transporting, concealing, dumping, leaving the victim at the crime scene or concealing the body at the primary crime scene … the fourth is essentially unheard of,' Arntfield said of Gacy's primary disposal method. 'There's a study on Hong Kong [murder], the victim goes down a flight of stairs in a carpet, there's no rivers to dump people in, so the victims are usually concealed in closets and places like that.' He added: 'In the U. S. that M. O. is almost unheard of.' Arntfield suggested that Gacy may have switched up his 'disposal methods' as he grew more comfortable with killing. 'I wonder if his disposal methods of various iterations devolves ... he would dump them somewhere first ... then got lazy and thought, "I'll kill them at the house," [when] the wife left, and then he started putting them in the river,' Arntfield said. 'There could be a methodology we don't know about. There could be dozens of unknown victims ... That to me is the question, from 1972 to 1975 he either didn't kill or must have had other improvised dump sites. He doesn't really settle on the crawl space until 1975 or 1976 and when that's filled, he turns to the water.'

Did Gacy change his methodology or perhaps his hunting territory? Retired Des Plaines detective Rafael Tovar has noted that, for a man in the seventies, John Wayne Gacy travelled a lot. Whether it was for business or pleasure, the killer admitted to being out of town every Sunday. Arntfield agrees: 'You have to look at that section – 1972 to 1975 – for a specific tally because we don't have the graveyard that was his house. He could have been on the road where he improvised.'

Bill Dorsch, a former Chicago cop, revealed in 1998 that there was a possibility Gacy may have buried victims on the grounds of an apartment building at 6114 West Miami Avenue in Chicago. In the years before he was arrested in 1978, Gacy had been in charge of maintenance at the building where his mother had lived after she moved out of the Norridge ranch house to make way for Carole Hoff. Dorsch lived close to the building and knew Gacy on a casual basis, enough to say, 'Hello. Nice weather we're having.' But Dorsch had spotted Gacy in the wee hours of the morning holding a shovel or a spade and digging trenches in the yard of the building. What could he be doing at that ungodly hour? Before the cop could ask what he was doing, Gacy spotted him and said, laughing as he did so, 'Bill, you know me, not enough hours in the day. You get it done when you can.' Dorsch later said after Gacy was arrested, he was left with the nagging question: What did he mean by 'get it done'. Get *what* done?

He told Cook County Sheriff's about the possible development. 'I thought, "If there's something there to follow up, they'll follow up,"' Dorsch told the news website Verge in 2012. But, it transpires, they never did. As a cop himself, Dorsch said he understood that his report was based on a hunch and that, in the massive, all-encompassing Gacy investigation, it may have been overlooked.

The retired cop later learned that several other West Miami Avenue residents told him they had seen Gacy digging trenches on the apartment grounds at times during the early to mid-seventies. One even said that the caretaker later put plants in the trenches that he had dug. Another watched Gacy lug a massive bag across the street.

Following pressure from an alternative Chicago newspaper and a website, officials finally submitted a request to excavate the grounds of the West Miami Avenue apartment. The state attorney scuttled the bid because of lack of probable cause. Then Sheriff Tom Dart filed a second request to excavate the grounds. It was granted in January 2013 and the search was slated for the spring. Using FBI cadaver dogs and high-tech radar, authorities began the search, largely in secrecy. The search revealed no evidence of human remains on the property. 'It's over,' *Chicago Sun-Times* columnist Michael Sneed wrote on 20 March 2013. 'There was no Geraldo moment. The search for victims of mass murderer John Wayne Gacy in the Northwest Side apartment building, where Gacy's mother once lived, turned up squat ... nothing. The elaborate, sophisticated search for more Gacy victims – conducted by Cook County Sheriff Tom Dart's office, and exclusively reported by Sneed months ago – was for naught.'

During the eighties, Gacy spoke to famed FBI profiler Robert Ressler. For his part, Ressler feared that there were unanswered questions in the Gacy investigation. He fell among those who believed Gacy had killed more than the thirty-three known victims. When Gacy travelled, Ressler believed, he killed – and killed in multiple states. Gacy would neither confirm nor deny the thesis in the days before his death. He merely smiled, as if saying, 'Figure it out.'

There are genuine reasons to believe that Gacy's victim count was higher than thirty-three. But what of the second major question that had plagued the investigation from the first day of the probe: had Gacy acted alone?

The hell-bound killer always blamed others, but in his typical bombastic fashion he overcooked his story. Almost immediately after his arrest, in December 1978, Gacy informed detectives that he had not acted alone in a number of the murders. He referred to his alleged accomplices as 'my associates' and asked whether they had been arrested. And when cops asked him if these 'associates' participated directly or indirectly in the murders, Gacy responded: 'Directly.' He pointed the finger at Michael Rossi and David Cram, two of his employees, who spent considerable time at Gacy's suburban home.

One investigator who wouldn't be named said there was 'overwhelming evidence Gacy worked with an accomplice'. Michael Arntfield essentially agrees. 'Over the last thirty-odd years we've been studying "team killers", and some of that research lends credence to the idea that Gacy had accessories,' he said, adding that if that's the case, the modus operandi might have been even more similar to the Houston serial killer Dean 'Candyman' Corll than thought. 'Dean Corll would conscript his victims to lure other victims until one of them ended up killing him after the brainwashing ended.'

Jeffrey Rignall testified that, on the night he was attacked by Gacy, there was a young man with brown hair watching as he was defiled by the barbaric contractor. The traumatised Rignall told cops he also saw a light flick on in another part of the house.

Just three days before the serial killer was arrested, when he was under round-the-clock surveillance, two detectives followed him into a Chicago watering hole. At the bar, Gacy met two of his employees, Rossi and another guy named Ed Hefner. The killer knew he was being watched and whisked the two out of earshot of the cops. As they returned to their table, Gacy was overheard telling the two: 'You'd better not let me down, you fuckers. You owe it to me.' There was mumbling that the detectives could not make out in response, but then they allegedly heard Rossi ask Gacy: 'And what? Buried like the other five?'

Michael Arntfield said it strains credulity, even if Rossi and Cram didn't take part in the murders, that they weren't aware of their boss's murderous predilections. 'There were the two guys working for Gacy's construction company and they would often flop at his house, one even lived there,' Arntfield said. 'There was no way they didn't know what was going on.'

However, he doesn't agree that this lets John Wayne Gacy off the hook. 'Does that change his culpability? No. But it opens up the question: What happened to these guys now? What are their movements, what corresponding crimes may they have been involved in such as child disappearances?' Arntfield said.

When Gacy spoke to Robert Ressler in the eighties, he told him that maybe 'two or three' employees who worked for P. D. M. had assisted in several of the grisly murders. And on death row, Gacy not only named Rossi and Cram but another former employee named Philip Paske. Paske was a known close associate and top lieutenant of a man named John David Norman. Norman was

Gacy's kind of guy. A violent paedophile who had sex-related convictions with young boys dating back to 1954 in Houston, Texas. During the early to late seventies, Norman gained notoriety for running a nationwide sex-trafficking operation called the Delta Ring. Based in Chicago, the ring supplied underage boys to older men – paedophiles. Norman would allegedly run ads for his operation that he called the Odyssey Foundation. Cops say he was always cruising for new talent. Two of the boys believed to have been slain by Gacy were last seen near Norman's home. This connection added gasoline to the burning theory that the contractor had connections to a sex-trafficking ring.

When he was arrested in Dallas in 1973, detectives discovered more than 30,000 index cards in Norman's home with the names of his paedophile clients along with their sexual preferences. 'He's the paedophile of paedophiles,' Dallas Police Detective Arsie Nelson said at the time. Accomplices of Dean Corll alleged that the Houston killer had worked with Norman and bought, sold and murdered many boys. The truth of these allegations has never been confirmed.

In a blockbuster story by the *Chicago Tribune* in 1976, a year after Norman was convicted, it was reported that Paske was Norman's closest friend and associate. The *Tribune* claimed that Paske had continued running Norman's ring after his arrest and said Paske himself was a convicted killer. Chicago's WGN-TV later obtained a note from Gacy that called Paske dangerous and said that he would 'pimp girls, boys, for sex or movies'.

'Gacy, Norman and Paske are all in Chicago around that time,' Tracy Ullman, a producer of *The Clown and the Candyman* documentary, told Oxygen.com. 'I find it hard for all these things to just be a coincidence.'

In the seventies, there was no internet for hook-ups or hunting, so paedophiles needed to have face-to-face contact with like-minded men. 'From years of research, we found that paedophiles – like Norman and Gacy – had lines of communication that tied them together, whether through coded ads in *Boy's Life* magazine or actual contact to trade pornography or traffic in humans,' Ullman said.

Michael Arntfield points to another similar case: 'The Oakland Child Killer case in Detroit in the 1970s is officially unsolved. We know now that there was a basic group of four local guys who had connections to this dead letter drop that received child porn. And eventually they made their fantasies a reality … In that era it seems that frequently, because of the secret society nature of paedophilia, that killers acted in teams.'

The 'secret society' nature of the operation meant not only that it was easy to access victims but that the victims were from a pool of marginalised people – the 'missing missing' as Arntfield termed them. He pointed to Canadian serial killer Bruce McArthur who murdered eight gay men, starting in 2010. McArthur selected highly vulnerable targets in the form of closeted gay men, largely from the Middle East. These men didn't want their families or friends to know about their sexuality so they would keep this side of their lives secret. It made it harder for cops to link them to McArthur. 'These secretive communities in which these predators can operate more efficiently offer a different climate or different circumstances that make it easier for killers,' Arntfield said. 'They were high facilitation victims whose lifestyles expose them to people like Bruce McArthur.' Gacy was a sadist who 'got off on screaming teenage boys', Arntfield argues. The rapes were secondary.

Gacy often maintained he wasn't even in Chicago when at least sixteen of the victims had vanished. And, in 2012, research by two Chicago lawyers revealed travel records that showed that Gacy was in fact in other states at the time of at least three of the murders that were pinned on him. In one instance, three days before the disappearance on 15 September 1977 of Robert Gilroy, Gacy had flown to Pittsburgh on Allegheny Airlines. The lawyers said Gacy returned to Chicago the day after Gilroy vanished.

There's further confusion around the disappearance of John Mowery. On 26 September 1977, travel records showed that Gacy was at a job site in Michigan at six a.m. It was the day after nineteen-year-old John Mowery had disappeared. Mowery had last been seen leaving his mother's house around ten p.m. the night before.

Mowery's roommate was a P. D. M. employee who formerly lived with John Wayne Gacy at the ranch house. The unidentified young man moved into Mowery's apartment less than a week before the disappearance. Two witnesses later told cops that the mystery roommate had suggested to Mowery that he meet 'a man who is going out of town' two days before Mowery was last seen.

One man who did not discount the lawyers' 2012 findings was Cook County Sheriff Tom Dart who was already behind renewed efforts to put names to the unidentified bodies unearthed from Gacy's crawl space more than forty years ago. There are still five nameless young men and boys in the graves marked only with their date of death and the words: 'We remembered'. Terry Sullivan, one of the prosecutors who sent Gacy to the death chamber, told the *Chicago Sun-Times*, 'I felt from the very beginning there may be loose ends.' The prosecutor was right. Even if those bodies are eventually identified there will be questions that continue to nag cops, survivors and the victims' families. John Wayne Gacy will remain as the protagonist in our most terrifying nightmares.

As this is written, the John Wayne Gacy investigation is still ongoing and there is no end in sight.